wisdom to
heal the earth

wisdom to heal the earth

Meditations & Teachings on the wisdom
of the Lubavitcher Rebbe,
RABBI MENACHEM M. SCHNEERSON
זצוקללה"ה נבג"מ זי"ע

BY TZVI FREEMAN
Author of Bringing Heaven Down To Earth

EZRA
PRESS

Published by Ezra Press
New York
5778 - 2018

In the beginning was everything.

Every voice that would ever be heard,

every daydream that would ever fleet through a distracted mind,

every furious wave of every stormy sea,

every galaxy that would ever erupt into being,

every gravitational field of every mass,

every charge of every electron,

the frantic ant running across the pavement beneath your feet,

the basket some kid scored in a park somewhere just now—

everything that ever would be and could be,

all cocooned within a single, deliberate and conscious thought.

And then that thought exploded.

to my mother,
may she continue to guide me.

foreword

Improving the world we live in has been a preoccupation of the Jewish people for millennia. Three times a day during the closing "*Aleinu*" prayer, Jews entreat that we fulfill our mission לתקן עולם, *l'taken olam*, "to perfect the world." Yet, in recent generations the pace of change has accelerated dramatically. It's as if the earth itself is seeking the fulfillment of its potential, once and for all.

Seeing new opportunities to improve and perfect the world everywhere, the Lubavitcher Rebbe, Rabbi Menachem M. Schneerson, of righteous memory, encouraged us to utilize all forms of technology to disseminate Jewish wisdom and values to all mankind.

Chabad.org therefore seeks to engage technology in every positive form and medium to empower Jews from all walks of life to understand and appreciate their 3,300-year-old tradition, and foster a deeper and more meaningful connection to Judaism, from the depths of its wisdom to its centrality in a life of practical action. We also demonstrate where and how the Torah's teachings can serve as an inspiration and guide to the non-Jewish world as well.

Today, the wisdom of the Torah travels at the speed of light, riding on fiber cables and surging through wireless space to teach, educate, nurture and connect the millions who study on Chabad.org each month.

Indeed, most of the ideas and words printed in this book were first published online on Chabad.org over the past decade. Yet even as we are committed to new media, books remain central to sharing the Torah's wisdom with the world.

Just as the printed word fills our physical space with wisdom in the form of tangible ink and paper, this book is meant to spur us to effect real change in our world.

It is our fervent prayer that very soon we will merit the coming of Moshiach, who will lead the world to its ultimate perfection, "perfecting the entire world, motivating all the nations to serve G-d together."

Chabad.org

20 Av, 5778
Brooklyn, NY

what is this book?

There are those who cling to the belief that we progress into a better future by treading over the dry bones of the past. This book is for those who have come to realize that everything that made that progress possible—everything most precious, most liberating and empowering, most meaningful and vital—was bequeathed to us by the most ancient traditions. Progress may be the child of innovation, but like a grand sequoia, it is ever-nurtured by its ancient roots.

If you want to push a boulder forward, you need first to ensure you're standing on solid ground. If you want to erect a tall building, first dig a deep foundation. If you want to build upon a healthy planet earth, first appreciate the depths of its ecology. If you want to create a healthy, resilient, and sustainable society, first understand the roots of our traditions, our narratives and our wisdom-teachings, and there you will find your vision of the future.

Everything here is based on the wisdom of the Lubavitcher Rebbe, Rabbi Menachem M. Schneerson, referred to by Jews everywhere as "the Rebbe." Rebbe means "my teacher." You'll find a short biography at the end of this book.

The Rebbe's teachings are firmly grounded in four thousand years of Jewish thought, sharply tuned to the needs of our time. He was a preeminent scholar in his generation in Talmud and Kabbalah, with a university education in science and technology. He was in constant touch with the pulse of the modern world, through his connections both with its leaders and with the common man and woman as well. He was a man beyond time and within it at once. He spoke with a sense of urgency and mission, with a message for all people, then and now.

And yet, most of his teachings remain inaccessible to most people. Which is what this book is attempting to correct.

That's also why this book contains few direct quotations. When the Rebbe spoke in public, he spoke in Yiddish, a language whose melodies, idioms and nuances defy translation. When he wrote, it was mostly in a complex and compact scholarly rabbinic Hebrew. Always, it was commentary on legacy texts—sometimes explicitly cited, more often not. The dots were left for you to connect; the most brilliant points were left for your pen to circle.

That's always been the way true wisdom has been transmitted—in such a form that a student can only extricate that wisdom by first mastering the background and context and then wrestling it to the ground, examining each word, and doing one's best to reconstruct the thought process that went through the teacher's mind.

There were teachings I had to study again and again for many years, tearing them apart in a struggle to understand what holds these pieces together, what the Rebbe is really getting at, and what all this is telling me, until finally, like a flash in the dark, the missing piece of the puzzle would appear, and all would fall into place. Then, or a few months later, I would attempt to condense what I had learned into as few words as possible, so I could carry it with me. That's how most of these meditations were born.

The introductory essays to each chapter, on the other hand, are a mix. Some are much the same as the meditations—presentations of the Rebbe's thoughts—but where more words are necessary. Others are meant to provide context to the meditations that follow, by presenting concepts essential to Chabad thought—such as *tikun, tzimtzum, birurim* and *neshamot.*

Some of these teachings are from the Rebbe's predecessors. That's because it's impossible to understand the Rebbe properly without a knowledge of the wisdom-tradition he follows. And, conversely, when we heard these teachings from the Rebbe, they shone with an entirely new light.

The Rebbe rarely discussed anything only one time. The references provided in the appendix are principally for those who want to explore a concept further, as well as for those who have difficulty believing that such radical ideas could come from a Chasidic leader.

Everything that's in this volume is available at Chabad.org. There, I hope to continue to update this work, as feedback comes in from my readers, and as I continue to meditate upon these teachings in my attempt to apply them in my own life.

Saying that this book is "by Tzvi Freeman" needs to be qualified. I've already told you that the teachings are not mine, but the Rebbe's—at least as I have understood them. Yaakov Ort acted as my editor, overseeing the project and providing invaluable comments throughout. It is rare to have an editor who both understands what you are trying to say and appreciates the way you want to say it. Rabbi Avraham Altein reviewed each chapter and provided his insights. This was a great privilege, as Rabbi Altein is a deep thinker and brilliant scholar in every field of Torah and especially in the Rebbe's teachings.

Rabbi Mendel Cohen of Yeshiva Ohr Elchanan, Los Angeles, copiously reviewed the manuscript, checking against the original sources and providing invaluable comments. These comments greatly contributed to the authenticity of the work.

And then there are those valuable readers who have provided feedback in their online comments. Those comments allow me to hear how my words are heard by many others, from many different directions.

Yet, most of all, it is the people at Chabad.org who made this book possible—management, all the staff, and certainly all our benefactors. Their dedication to making the Rebbe's vision real by teaching Torah wisdom and encouraging real-time *mitzvot* has been essential to the creation of this work for more than a decade. Somehow, I have been privileged to take some small part in the most visited Jewish information site on the world wide web, extraordinary in the breadth and depth of its content, continually monitored and updated by a team of over 50 dedicated programmers, designers, writers, editors, expert responders and other support staff.

I carry a deep sense of gratitude to every member of that staff, to our director, Rabbi Zalman Shmotkin, and to our supporters, as Chabad.org has stood by my side all these years, enabling me to continue in my writing, and making it possible to reach my audience through an ever-growing variety of media. Each one of those individuals is represented herein, and each one can take pride in its success.

To all, please accept my gratitude and thanks.

—Tzvi Freeman

table of contents

———◆———

———◆———

wisdom to
heal the earth

tikun

Maybe you've heard of *tikun olam*. It's a phrase thrown around a lot in Jewish circles.

Olam means world, and *tikun*—well, it means all sorts of things. But in this sense, it means "to repair and improve."

So *tikun olam* means "repairing and improving the world," which is what we're here to do.

Because, in case you didn't notice, the world is broken. Even the stuff that looks great isn't anywhere near what it's supposed to be.

Some people say, "That's just the way things are. Live with it."

Others say, "Let the One who made it fix it."

And yet others say, "Escape it."

But Jews say, "Fix it. Whatever you can. Leave behind a better world. Because that's what you're here for."

◆

Where did we get such a crazy idea?

Maybe it's from Genesis, where it says we were "placed in the garden to serve it and protect it."

Or from the ancient Midrash that says, "Everything G-d created in His world was designed to be improved."

But, in most part, the way we think of *tikun olam* today is the end-product of a chain with three crucial links—three Jewish revolutionaries of the spirit: Rabbi Yitzchak Luria, Rabbi Yisrael Baal Shem Tov, and Rabbi Schneur Zalman of Liadi.

Each answered a question. Each answer brought us closer to how we think now.

Ari means "lion." That's the title universally granted to Rabbi Yitzchak Luria. He taught for less than three years in Tzfat, in the Galilean hills of Northern Israel, before his early passing in 1572. Few people have had such impact in such a brief time.

The Ari taught in esoteric terms, employing rich metaphor in complex detail. But if we distill it down, through many distillations, we can tell a story something like this:

In the beginning there shone an infinite light. But within an infinite light there can be no finite world.

So the light receded, remaining infinite, but creating a vacuum. Absolute darkness.

And then, from the infinite light beyond and into the darkness within burst a fine, measured beam of light. A ray of conscious thought. An idea. A ray that held everything—

all of time and all of space, all wisdom and all understanding of that wisdom, all greatness and might, beauty and glory, wonder and creativity—

every voice that would ever be heard, every daydream that would fleet through a distracted mind, every furious wave of a stormy sea, every galaxy that would erupt into being, every charge of every electron, the frantic ant running across the pavement beneath your feet, the basket some kid scored in a park somewhere just now—everything that ever would be and could be—

all cocooned within a single, deliberate and conscious thought.

An intense thought. So intense, that each concept it held left no room for anything other than itself.

Which is why that thought is called the *World of Tohu*—meaning: a world of confusion. A world comparable to the emotions of a child—when there is love, there is no room for disdain; when there is anger, there is no room for understanding; when there is self, there is no room for other. A world, as the *Zohar* describes, where each entity is a king, and no other entity is allowed entry until that king dies.

In the language of Kabbalah: Wisdom left no space for Understanding, and Understanding had no room for Wisdom. Kindness left no space for Judgment, and Judgment had no room for Kindness. Each concept was a world of its own, a totality that neither needed nor could bear anything outside of itself. All were ideals. Nowhere was there harmony.

And so that thought exploded.

The explosion gave birth to many worlds. Worlds of *Tikun*. Each world repaired itself, creating its own harmony.

Until it came to our world. In our world, the most vital fragments of Tohu are found, those that the higher worlds were not capable of harmonizing. That was left up to us. Our souls were placed within bodies in this world to perform the ultimate repair.

———◆———

You've heard of a primal explosion before—the Big Bang. But here we are talking about more than matter and energy.

The universe contains conscious beings, such as ourselves. From where does that consciousness emerge, if not from the very fabric of the universe itself?

So think of a primal, singular, deliberate and conscious thought, too intense to contain itself. What happens when such an idea, rather than gradually developing and expanding, chaotically explodes?

Imagine taking a book and casting the words and letters into the air.

Imagine an orchestra where none of the musicians can hear one another, and the conductor is nowhere to be found.

Imagine a movie set without a director, each actor speaking lines without a clue of their meaning.

That is our world. A book in search of its meaning, an orchestra in search of its score, actors in search of their playwright and director.

Awaiting us to rediscover that meaning. To put Humpty Dumpty back together again.

The fragments of that shattered origin are called sparks. They are the divine meaning of each thing—their place and particular voice in the great symphony.

Each spark is trapped within a shell. They are the noise and dissonance that shrouds those sparks when they are thrown violently from their place.

Our job is to see past the shell and discover the spark within. And then to reconnect that spark to its place in that grand original vision.

We call that purification. And the result is called *geulah*—liberation.

The liberation of humankind is intimately tied to the liberation of those sparks of meaning. Your personal liberation is tied to the particular sparks assigned to your soul.

Once a critical mass of sparks has been reconnected, the entire world is liberated. It becomes a different world. An improved world. Because only through that shattering and reconnecting do the parts find their harmony.

This was all very counter-intuitive for a lot of people.

Both religion and philosophy had allotted human beings a passive role in their world's destiny. The Creator had made a beautiful world, we had messed it up. It was up to Him to judge, reward, punish, and take care of our mess.

And now that was reversed. The Creator was the One who had handed us a mess—so that we could complete the job of perfecting it from within. It is a good world, a very good world—essentially because we are empowered to make it good.

Effectively, the Ari gave center-stage to the actions of human beings.

The idea of *tikun* seeped rapidly into every facet of Jewish thought and affected every Jewish movement, directly or indirectly. Jews no longer saw themselves as passive servants of G-d's judgment, but as active players, whose redemption, and the redemption of the entire world—indeed, the entire cosmos—lay in their hands.

Every mitzvah they did gained new meaning. Every prayer, every word of Torah study—each was now not just a good deed to be rewarded, but another step towards the ultimate *geulah* of the entire world.

The Ari was a halachist—an expert and authority in Jewish law—

and he saw all of Jewish practice as a crystallization of Kabbalah. *Tikun* in action.

The idea of *tikun* also spread to the intelligentsia of 17th century Europe, who were fascinated with all things Hebrew, and especially the Kabbalah. It was at that time that people first began to speak in terms of human progress, of building a better world through social action and advances in the natural sciences.

As historians have pointed out, it is difficult to identify any source for these notions—certainly not in Greco-Roman philosophy, nor in the doctrines of the Reformation—nowhere other than the Kabbalah, and specifically the teachings of the Ari.

The idea of *tikun* entered the world through the Ari, but it remained the property of mystics and masters. It was widely misunderstood, distorted, and even abused. It took another 170 years before it gained practical application in the life of the everyman.

Rabbi Israel ben Eliezer is popularly known as the Baal Shem Tov ("Master of a Good Name"). He taught that every person is a master of *tikun* in his or her own world.

Not only the seeker and the scholar, but also the simple farmer and the busy merchant. Even the small child.

By his time, the greatest Talmudic scholars and rabbinic leaders were deeply immersed in the teachings of the Ari. But many of them also believed the only way to fix the human body was by breaking it—by fasting and punishing it. And the way to teach the common people was by breaking their spirit, instilling in them a fear of hell.

The Baal Shem Tov provided a subtle but landmark shift of emphasis. It was less about breaking the shell and more about embracing the fruit—and letting the shell fall away on its own.

To the Baal Shem Tov, *tikun* meant finding the good wherever it could be found and celebrating it. His disciples would wander from town to town, observing the heartfelt prayers, the sincere *mitzvot* and the good deeds of the simple folk, and telling them how much G-d cherished them and their deeds.

Wherever a soul travels in this world, the Baal Shem Tov taught, it is led there to find sparks that have been waiting since the time of Creation for this soul to arrive. Without realizing it, this precious soul is purifying the world, with its deeds and words.

Rabbi Schneur Zalman of Liadi lived—as most Jews of the time—in Eastern Europe. Yet the reverberations of the French Revolution rung throughout his world.

Rabbi Schneur Zalman was also a revolutionary, but a traditional one. More than anyone, he was responsible for conveying the teachings of the Baal Shem Tov into the modern world.

Strange as it may sound, by grounding the teachings of the Ari and the Baal Shem Tov in Midrash and Talmud, and ultimately in the language of Jewish practice, he turned the spiritual quest of humankind on its head.

Our mission in life, he taught, is not to get to heaven. Or to become heavenly beings. It is to bring heaven down to earth.

Earth—not the worlds of angels or the worlds of souls or some reified, divine world of light—but this material world where darkness reigns and truth is hidden. This is the place where the Grand Artist wants to be found.

*From the beginning of creation, G-d's presence was
principally in our world, the lowest world.*

—*Shir Hashirim Rabbah 5:1.*

*Before G-d created this world, He created worlds and
destroyed them, created worlds and destroyed them.
He said, "These I don't like. These I don't like." Then He
created this world. He said, "This one I like."*

—*Bereishit Rabbah 3:9.*

*Since the time the world was created, G-d desired that
He should have a home among us, the lower beings.*

—*Midrash Tanchuma, Nasso 7:1.*

Why would an omnipotent G-d will to dwell in darkness? What desire could He have in a place where He is found only through painful struggle and dogged effort?

The answer is in the process of *tikun* itself:

What happens as we succeed, as we collect those letters and string them back together to form their original words and sentences?

Their collective meaning begins to reappear. A story begins to unfold. An underlying harmony, a symphony—not of our invention, but of our discovery.

What happens when the darkness opposes us? When we persist despite all the lies it spews at us? When we refuse to surrender because we have faith in a deeper truth?

Then a yet deeper light is revealed. One the Author could not say. One that could only be discovered through our stubborn faith and toil.

That is the ultimate light, greater than that which shone at the very beginning. Because we have grabbed the darkness by its neck and forced it to shine more truth than any light could shine.

In effect, the primal thought from which this world was conceived has dissected itself, discovered itself, and put itself back together again.

Tikun, then, does not mean merely repair. In fact, throughout early Jewish literature it rarely does. It means to improve. To fix.

Because in that process, the story discovers not only its own meaning and its own beauty; it discovers its Author. The very essence of its Author that could not be expressed in any spiritual world.

Where? Within itself. Its darkest self.

When you trace *tikun olam* back to its source, you get a whole new picture of what it means. It turns out to be far more revolutionary than you would have imagined.

Tikun olam is about much more than justice and an end to suffering. Those are symptoms. *Tikun* means to fix the cause.

The cause is that we don't know where we are.

We think we are in a world that just is. Or some dark hole to escape.

The first and last step of our *tikun* is to awaken to the realization that we are actors in a great drama, players in a master symphony. That we are here with a mission, accountable to a Higher Consciousness that brought this place into being.

With that awakening alone, the world would be redeemed.

With that awakening alone, we would discover that we never left the Garden. We only lost awareness of where we stand.

We stand within infinite light. For even the darkness is light.

1

leave nothing behind

If it is permissible, we must use it for good.
If it can be raised higher, we cannot leave it below.
If it has become trapped in sinister darkness, the means
will come to liberate it from there.

For everything He made, He made with purpose.

what can i fix?

Rabbi Shimon Bar Yochai hid from the Romans in a cave for thirteen years. There, he was visited by heavenly beings, by Elijah the Prophet, and even by Moses. It was there that he composed the holy *Zohar*.

When he left the cave and came to a town, he did not say, "Let me enlighten you with the inner light of Torah, the light that has been hidden since the six days of creation."

He said, "What is there in your town that I can help fix?" And the people presented him with a communal issue that required his sage advice.

Whatever knowledge you are given in this world, whatever wisdom, enlightenment, or inspiration, it is all only and exclusively for one purpose: To assist you in fixing this world.

3

the taller they are...

You might think that divine sparks are meted out by simple protocol: The lowlier the creation, the lowlier the divine spark it holds.

Just the opposite: Only the highest sparks could descend to the lowest places and retain their power to sustain a being.

Those are the sparks remaining to be rescued today. Those are the sparks that squeeze out our deepest powers to rescue them from the mud. And through them, the ultimate light is revealed.

inside job

Fixing up the world is always an inside job.

What do we fix? That which we need.

When do we fix anything? When we are in need.

Why do we need anything? Because it awaits us to fix it.

Because our destiny is tied to the destiny of that which we repair and improve.

So it is with the food we eat, the bodies in which we live, the business in which we work, and the community in which we live. You can only rescue the divine spark within a thing when you have a stake in it, when your entire being is tied up with it.

Nobody can come from the outside, stay outside, and make real, lasting, beneficial change.

a sign from below

How do you know what you are meant to fix?

If you have a real need for this thing, then you know it awaits you to carry it to a higher place.

if it's broken...

If you see something that is broken, fix it.

If you cannot fix all of it, fix some of it.

But do not say there is nothing you can do. Because, if that were true, why would this broken thing have come into your world?

Did the Creator then create something for no reason?

top down, ground up

Entering within, there are two paths of healing before you: From the top down or from the ground up.

Working top-down, you see nothing but good, you do nothing but kindness, and you spread wisdom and light everywhere. The divine, lost sparks are drawn to you as to a magnet, leaping into the fire of their own accord, consumed in totality. All is transformed.

But it does not last. The sparks dance only to the light of your fire; as soon as it begins to fade, they fall back to their places. The darkness returns, perhaps yet more powerful, due to the nurture you have provided.

Working from the ground up, you enter within the world that holds those sparks in captivity and become part of it.

You do not ignore the beast within you; you recognize it, speak with it, coaxing it to look up to the heavens and discover that it is not the sum total of all that is.

You do not ignore the world around you; you deal with it head-on, on its own terms. Only that "all your deeds are for the sake of heaven," and "in all your ways, you know Him." Meaning: They are **your** ways, the ways of a created being—yet in them you know **Him**, the Creator of being.

This transformation is real and lasting, because it comes from within, and through hard labor.

dual peace

True, when we work from above and stay above, the transformation you effect does not last. Yet, while it is there, it is all-consuming. While it is there, everything experiences a whole new state of being.

True, when we work from within, the transformation is self-sustaining. But it is only skin deep. The beast within remains a beast, just slightly more enlightened. The world remains a world, only a brighter world.

Ultimately, both approaches are needed. We can teach and provide knowledge, yet preserve a sense of the transcendent and unknowable. We can work with the world on its own terms, but we must show it that it is only a world. Within a higher context, it is nothing at all.

Until, eventually, that beast and the world will become the devices through which an unknowable G-d can be known.

redeemed in peace

There is a third strategy. It is powered by the intense light of inner Torah that awakens the essence-core of your soul, a place so deep that it knows no change, it does not move and cannot be broken.

When that essence-core awakens from its slumber, the essence of all things also breaks out from its absolute darkness into the light. Even the darkness emerges as light.

There is no longer war, but peace. No more opponents, only allies.

To the essence of your soul, after all, is tied the essence of all that is. Even of the darkness.

tied to the source

There are places where you cannot go on your own accord.

To enter into the depths and stay connected above, to hide under cover of darkness and be there a source of light, to journey to the enemy side and return in peace— all this is only possible if you are tied and bonded with a *tzaddik*.

You must be sent there by someone for whom this cavern does not exist; someone for whom the darkness is already light.

where you cannot go

How can you know if you can lift this place up, or if it will pull you down?

Because we have a Torah, and the Torah is our guide. And we have sages of Torah, and they can instruct us. If the Torah says you must go, you must go. If the Torah says you cannot go, you cannot go.

No matter how great an opportunity it may seem, no matter how fantastic the immediate rewards may appear, you will not redeem the sparks. Without the Torah's permission, you will only further empower the darkness that holds this place captive.

nothing higher

There are things you fix by doing with them the right thing. Those carry your soul high.

There are things you fix by not doing with them the wrong thing. Those carry your soul higher than high.

Then there are things you fix because you did the wrong thing with them, and then you regretted that with all your heart and turned your life around. Those carry your soul high beyond imagination.

Yet all this is speaking of forbidden things, things that have some reality of their own, and perhaps even some means by which they could be used for good—only that you may or may not have used them that way.

There are, however, things in this world that are only evil, whose entire being is but to oppose all that is good—to strike fear, to cause despair, to be darkness. To deny reality.

And so in your denial of their reality, in your refusal to show them fear, to provide them any ounce of credibility, they dissipate into the nothingness they truly are.

Those carry your soul to her very core and being. And yet higher.

13

choose your strategy

How do you fix a place, a problem, a person—anything at all?

By rejecting the bad and embracing the good.

If so, you have two possible strategies:

You could focus on all that is bad, ugly, and diseased, scraping it away and chasing it out, so that, eventually, all that's left is pure and healthy.

Or you could focus on whatever is still healthy and functional, embracing it, fortifying it, and using it for its true purpose, so that, eventually, the dark crust in which it was imprisoned simply falls away.

Certainly, both strategies are necessary, and both have their time and place. But where do you begin?

It depends. When the human soul shines bright and strong, when only a few details are out of place—then you can focus on discarding whatever bad remains.

But when everything is a mess, when the soul lies deep in coma, when contagion has overcome every cell—then to attack the disease head-on could prove fatal. Then you have no choice but to seek out the precious sparks of life that have survived. Fan those embers and let them heal all else.

soul fixing

How will you fix a soul?

A soul doesn't need fixing. She needs to be uncovered. Sometimes she needs to be dug out of the ashes. But the soul remains a pure, whole gem.

Dig deeply and deeper yet, sift through the darkened embers, search for a spark that still shines. Fan that spark until a flame appears, find the mitzvah that will serve as its oil and wick. Until all is consumed in the warmth of that flame.

For compassion is the redeemer of love, and love is the mother of all good deeds.

rewrite

There are no things. There are only words. The divine words of creation telling a story, calling all into being.

The words become scattered and we no longer understand their meaning. They appear to us static and meaningless. As things. But they are not things. They are words in exile.

If so, their redemption lies in the story we tell with them.

Joy can create one story. Inspiration yet another. Reach to the divine spark within you, and a whole new story emerges.

What story will you tell with the scattered fragments of your life?

reporting

He doesn't need you to report on the dirt in His world.
He knows quite enough about it, for He put it there—and
not because He has an interest in it.

He sent you here to search out the jewels hidden in the
mud, clean them and polish them until they shine.

And when you bring them to Him, the angels make
a crown of them for Him, and say, "Look what Your
children have made for You from the mud!"

inventions

In the beginning, G-d spoke. And whatever He spoke crystallized into material form.

But what about that which He did not speak?

Those waited for the human mind to bring them into being.

When the human being first harnessed fire and bred animals and crops, he simply acted out a divine unspoken thought. The same with those inventors who developed the steam engine, the electric turbine, the radio, and the digital computer. Each creation makes its appearance at the appropriate time, all as choreographed from the beginning of time.

All that G-d made, He made only for His glory, including these. They, too, are vitalized by a spark of the divine. And it is up to us to liberate that spark and reconnect it to its origin, as it is found in the context of the Creator's original plan.

18

whose job

Prayer, meditation, acts of kindness—those all fulfill our needs. We need air, we need water, we need to stay connected with our Source above.

Your work, your family, your path in the world—those fulfill a Divine desire. It is He who wishes to find a home in this world He has made.

19

room for
inspiration

Yesterday, you were inspired. Today, that is all gone. And so, you are depressed.

But this is the way life moves forward:

Everything begins with inspiration. And then the inspiration steps aside, to make room for you to bring it into action. For fire to become deeds.

the soul grows up

This soul of yours, ultimately she finds there is something even more momentous than herself. There is her purpose.

To accomplish, to heal, to fix the world—these, she discovers, take precedence over her thirst to return to her womb, to bask in the divine light from which she came.

In that moment of discovery she graduates from being G-d's little child to becoming one with His very being.

descending to ascend

The mess of fragments the Creator gave us, those are the pieces He broke apart for us to create our own, better world.

But the mess of fragments we have torn apart ourselves by our own poor choice—who is to say that these too have any redeeming value?

Because this is the way the world was designed: Any descent will eventually result in an ascent. The more broken the world, the better it can be put back together. Yes, a more arduous job on a longer, winding road—but eventually it will be achieved.

Wherever you are, in whatever situation you have gotten yourself, there is purpose, only one purpose: To go higher.

write your own script

You came on stage with a script in your hand. The script tells of you, the hero of the story, bringing light into places of darkness, repairing that which is broken, healing that which has fallen ill, creating beauty from scattered fragments of everyday life.

Your soul is tied to that script. Without it, you have no reason to be here. For you were conceived within that context, born to fill that role.

And should you fail to perform according to script, what then?

Then you must write your own script, one that can heal even that which you yourself have broken. A script that can get this story back on track, but this time through a labor of love that belongs to you alone.

And your Creator who conceived you and conceived this entire plan, what will He think of this new script you have composed?

He will laugh in delight, exclaiming, "Look at my child! She has written her own script!"

insider's history

The history of humankind is not about the rise and fall of empires, nor about their wars and conquests. It is about a different sort of battle, the battle over whether the Creator of this place belongs here below or in some heaven above.

Those who believe He belongs in His heavens destroy the earth. Those who believe He belongs on earth build heaven here.

That is the battle each one of us fights, and that is the story of all humanity's journey. And that is all that really matters. For that is all there is to any human being.

life's memories

This experience, to give life, to watch it grow, to be torn apart by it, to receive pleasure from it, and to give life again—for this the soul descended from her ethereal heights.

And when it shall return to that origin, enveloped in these memories, it will finally know their depth. And, with them, travel ever higher and yet higher.

radical reversal

Before the beginning, there was nothing but light. Infinite light. The notion of a world was absurd. Even a brilliant, shining, glorious world would be fully consumed within the intensity of that light, a light that knew no bounds.

So He hid the light. All of it. There was absolute darkness.

And now there could be a world.

How does darkness allow a world? Because in darkness you know only yourself.

When there is light, you see that you stand within a greater whole, that you are only a small being, a single iteration of that whole. When you feel the primal light that projects you into being, your very sense of self begins to dissolve. Within infinite light, you are not a thing at all.

But in darkness, a world can exist; a world that can say, "I am."

And it does. To the point that it cannot imagine anything other than its own existence.

In effect, a radical reversal has occurred. The background has become foreground, and the foreground has become background. The light has receded into darkness, and the darkness has become the energy of being. Before, it was impossible to imagine a world. Now it is impossible to imagine anything but world. This world.

Which is all good, very good.

Return to that radical first step towards our creation. What came before the darkness?

"When the King first desired a world," says the *Zohar*, "He engraved its forms in the pure supernal light."

The *Zohar* speaks in rich metaphor. It asks us to imagine engravings within pure light—that which can neither be seen nor known. Until the light is dismissed.

Think of a program for existence etched into a bright sky, engulfed within endless light, but there, nonetheless, containing all that would ever be, awaiting its birth, its chance to become real.

With the removal of that infinite light, a trace of those engravings remained. And now a trickle of light burst through from beyond into the darkness, from a place where this great vacuum had never occurred, where it remained an absurdity, where there was still nothing but the infinite light.

As an electric force propels static code to dance and play upon your screen, so this stream of light breathed life into that trace left behind, those formulas and patterns, so that they became a reality, and began to tell their story.

What is our place in this story?

It is to latch onto that trickle of light and draw more and yet more into this darkness. Until the darkness is flooded with light.

For this, we were given a Torah of light, with deeds prescribed to transform the darkness. Because the Torah comes to us from the very origin of that stream of light, from the bowels of the fountain from which it flows.

Our role is to reverse the reversal. To create something yet more radical:

To make a world that is surprised at its own existence. A world that says, "Isn't it wondrous that I am? That a rotting seed yields a great oak out of sunlight and thin air; that a newborn child cries out to catch its first breath; that a whole new world of life is reborn at every moment when there is no reason that anything should be? Isn't it wondrous that there is anything at all?"

Where once the light was the domain of prophets and lofty souls, attained by solitude and revelation, in the high places and the courtyards and chambers of the Holy Temple, there will be a world where "your sons and daughters will prophesy," where even "the physical eye will see" that there is nothing else but G-d.

The light will become the obvious reality—the natural state of life. As for this world, it will be a perpetual wonder.

This answers a tough question: If the darkness was meant to be flooded with light, what was the point? We will simply return to where we started, when there was nothing but the infinite light.

No, there is no return. For two reasons.

First, because now there is already a world. And this world will remain. There will be a world, and the world will be filled with infinite light. Because it is through our efforts in this world that this infinite light has come to shine within it.

Second, because this infinite light will reflect a much deeper reality. The initial infinite light told of a Creator who is a source of light. But this new light will tell of a Creator of darkness and light, world and not world, being and not being. All of these can coincide and find union in His presence, for He knows no bounds.

We are almost there. Keep tugging on that stream of light. Just one more tug...

———◆———

nothing else

Deep in meditation, the mind's eye catches a glimmer of light.

A glimmer of light from G-d. But for one who seeks G-d Himself, the light is not G-d.

Secluded from the business of humankind and earthly pleasures, immersed in knowledge of the higher realms, there comes a day when the prophet hears with his ears the voice that brings all into being; sees with his eyes the splendor of that light.

A splendorous light from G-d. But the light is not G-d.

In a time to come, every small child will see more than the greatest prophet could ever imagine, the physical eye will perceive more than any soul has ever known, there will be a world, and its entire being will be a means to know its Creator—so much so that the very stones of the earth will scream out, "There is nothing else but He!"

That is G-d.

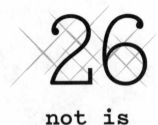

not is

How could it be?

How could a human ego know it is nothing but a figment of a greater mind—and yet remain a human being?

How could a physical eye see infinite light—and yet remain an eye?

How could a stone scream out that there is nothing else but G-d—and yet remain a stone?

It must be that the true reality of all things is not to be, but to know.

There is nothing else but knowing that there is nothing else but G-d.

unmasked

As impossible as it sounds, as absurd as it may seem—
the mandate of darkness is to become light; the mandate
of a busy, messy world is to find oneness.

We have proof, for the greater the darkness becomes and
the greater the confusion of life, the deeper our souls
reach inward to discover their own essence-core.

How could it be that darkness leads us to find a deeper
light? How could confusion lead us to find a deeper
truth?

Only because the very act of existence was set from its
beginning to know its own Author.

As it says, "In the beginning...G-d said, 'It shall become
light!'"

present in absence

The true teacher is most present in his absence.

It is then that all he has taught takes root, grows and blossoms.

The student despairs for his teacher's guidance, and in that yearning, the student leaves behind his old way of thinking. His mind opens to receive all that his teacher gave him, to think as his teacher thought, to know as his teacher knew.

29

light forever

At the threshold of liberation, darkness filled the land of Egypt. Yet in the homes of those to be liberated, there was only light.

Light is our true place and light is our destiny. As dawn approaches, darkness shakes heaven and earth in the final throes of its demise. But those who belong to light and cleave to it with all their hearts have nothing to fear.

Even as they fall into the deepest caverns where no stone glimmers, no path yields promise, and all meaning seems unfathomable, even there that light will lead them. It will reveal to them the treasures that lie there, which they must rescue for their own liberation.

All is truly light.

For darkness is created to die, but light is forever.

30

times are changing

The times in which we live are not ordinary times.

Everything is suddenly changing, rearranging itself. Technology leaps ahead daily, affecting the way we do things, how we communicate, our concept of life and the universe.

While an old world struggles to cling to its self-defeating patterns, the stage is set for a world as it is meant to be.

31

the goal

Time began. So we are told in the first phrase of our Torah. Today, the hard data of astronomers and physicists concurs. As impossible as it is to imagine, all we know of—space, time, the very nature of things—all has a beginning.

And it has a goal, an ultimate state. Every era, every event, every moment through which time passes is a step closer to that goal.

32

the drama

All the cosmos came to be because G-d chose
to invest His very essence into a great drama:
The drama of a lowly world becoming the home
of an infinite G-d. A marriage of opposites, the
fusion of finite and infinite, light and darkness,
heaven and earth.

We are the players in that drama, the cosmic
matchmakers. With our every action, we have
the power to marry our mundane world to the
Infinite and Unknowable.

the game

Like a matching game, each act of beauty uncovers another face of the infinite. Each generation completes its part of the puzzle.

Until the table is set and prepared. Until all that remains is for the curtains to be raised, the clouds to dissipate, the sun to shine down on all our bruised and bloodied hands have planted, and let it blossom and bear fruit.

That is where we are now. We know a world in the process of becoming. Soon will be a world where each thing has arrived.

cutting off the supply

To fight evil face-to-face is futile. But we can cut off its supply.

Between good and evil lies a neutral ground, a battlefield—the realm of all things permissible. All supplies to the enemy must pass through this realm. Because evil has no power of its own—it lives entirely off the scraps thrown to it from above.

By taking all that is permissible and using it only for good, honestly and uprightly, with purpose that transcends our own selves, the supply lines are broken.

When every activity of life becomes a way to know G-d, evil simply withers away and dies.

35

completion

Through many journeys through many lives, each of us will find and redeem all the divine sparks in our share of the world.

Then the darkness that holds such mastery, such cruelty, such irrational evil that it contains no redeeming value—all this will simply vanish like a puff of steam in the midday air.

As for that which we salvaged and used for good, it will shine an awesome light never known before.

The world will have arrived.

36

finally winning

Throughout history, countless tactics and strategies are played in the battle over Creation's destiny. But at the end of the day, the only thing that really matters is winning, and winning comes at the very end.

With every passing round of the game, the soul puts out whatever she has. When it comes to the last stretch, neck and neck with the enemy, she has to do better than that. Her very core ignited, she bursts into an explosion of power never before imagined.

This is the stubborn power we have today, to finally change the world and transform it into a G-dly place. Not with our own strength, but with the power of all those before us. Because now, from above, every power is released; the very essence is called forth. To win.

37

longing for spring

Cultivate the soul with hope; teach her to await the break of dawn.

Through its ordeals, the earth is softened to absorb the rains. Yet it still must hope—for this is a Spring that comes for those who long for it.

And so the Sages say, "In the merit of hope, our parents were redeemed from Egypt."

38

technology

Technology is not here simply to provide utility. It is also meant as a springboard to wonder, allowing us to conceive our reality in ways previously unimaginable. It provides an ever-expanding bank of metaphor to crystallize the most abstract ideas into tangible forms.

Don't think that this is a mere side-benefit of technology. On the contrary, for this purpose these ideas were embedded into the universe from the six days of creation, only to be unfolded in our times.

39

treasure island

Our souls are in exile within our bodies. Our nation is in exile within a foreign world.

Therefore, there are two things we must know:

That this is not our place.

And that hidden treasure lies buried here, for G-d dwells in darkness.

If we only remember that this is not our place, we may remain strong, and we may even shine in the darkness. But what profit will there be from our exile?

And if we only remember that treasure lies here, we will begin to believe that this is our place, and, if so, of what use is the treasure?

fearless

*G-d said to Jacob: I am the G-d of your fathers. Do not
fear descending to Egypt....*

—Genesis 46:3

The pain is real. The fear is not.

The pain is real, because we are not in our true place. Nothing is in
its true place. It is called exile.

The fear is not real, because no matter where we are, our G-d is
still with us.

The only thing we have to fear is that we may no longer feel the
pain. For it is that pain of knowing we are in the wrong place that
lifts us higher, beyond this place.

41

redeeming hope

One who has given up hope is without a G-d.

One who awaits liberation each day is already free.

42

pity on the cosmos

To the Rebbe, the exile of the Shechinah was a painful reality of desperate urgency. To the rest of us, well, we have other concerns. Again and again, the Rebbe struggled to bring us to his perspective, and to place the responsibility to change the world firmly in our hands:

Perhaps, for you, this exile is not so bad. And you feel you are doing whatever you can about it, anyway.

But it is not just you alone in exile. Abraham, Isaac, and Jacob, and all the generations of their children, as well as all the heavenly host—in fact, the entire Creation—are all unfulfilled, in exile and imprisoned. Even the Creator locks Himself into prison along with His Creation.

Until you get us out of here.

cosmic marriage

From the moment that they were sundered apart, the earth has craved to reunite with heaven; physical with spiritual, body with soul, the life that breathes within us with the transcendental that lies beyond life, beyond being.

And yet more so does the Infinite Light yearn to find itself within that world, that pulse of life, within finite, earthly existence. There, more than any spiritual world, is the place of G-d's delight.

Towards this ultimate union, all of history flows, all living things crave, all of human activities are subliminally directed. When it will finally occur, it will be the quintessence of every marriage that has ever occurred.

May it be soon in our times, sooner than we can imagine.

the ultimate delight

What is G-d's ultimate delight?

That a human soul will build portals of light so that the Creator's presence may shine into His creation.

That a breath from His essence will pull herself out of the mud and turn to Him in love.

That a child of His being, exiled to the shadows of a physical world, will discover that the darkness is nothing more than Father hiding, waiting for His child to discover Him there.

But none of these can reach to the essence of all delights, the origin of all things, the hidden pleasure beyond all pleasures:

The delight that this breath, this soul, this child did it all on her own.

45

earned living

All that can be cherished from this world,
All that makes life worth living,
Is that which is mined from its bowels through your own toil,
Fashioned from its clay by your own craft,
Fired in the kiln of your own heart.

The exhilaration that awaited you at the summit of your most
grueling climb.

That for which you bruised your hands and wearied your limbs,
For which you beat back the beast inside you,
For which you defied a mocking world.

Oh, how precious, how resplendent a feast,
a life forged by the hands of its own master!

hiding destiny

How did He make a world?

First, He thought to Himself, "I desire light. I desire love. I desire acts of kindness and beauty." And He saw that this was good.

Then He put aside that light. As a person who puts aside his dreams so that he can begin the work that will make them possible, so the Creator put aside the vision He first desired.

And He made a world. As though that was the whole point—a world for the sake of being a world.

Only much later in the story did someone hear a whisper, "Do you know the real purpose for which I made this world?"

Now you know why reality is hard and love is soft,
Why apathy flows with ease while kindness must climb mountains,
Why light is always the intruder upon the boundless empire of darkness.

And yet, in the end, light is the hidden destiny of all that is.

open your eyes

This goal, when will we reach it?

It was once far, but now it is near.

When will we hold it in our hands?

When we will open our eyes to see
it is already here.

darkness speaks

The Kabbalists call it the primal *tzimtzum*. *Tzimtzum* means a reduction, but this first *tzimtzum* was much more. It was a total and complete reversal of the previous state, from a state of infinite light to an utter void.

And it is the origin of everything that would ever go wrong. Of every sin, every evil. Every darkness.

If some light had been left, darkness would never have had a chance. A trickle of light, even ever so slender and faint, would have projected a magnificent universe into being, a universe without confusion, of perfect harmony with its origin, as the fidelity of light to its source. A universe where nothing would ever be broken.

But instead, He chose to first remove all light, to create an utter void, and only then to pierce that void, to invade the realm of absolute darkness with a finely measured sliver of light. From this point on, all that would be created would first shatter before it could be repaired.

Why did He remove all light? Why did He choose that things could go wrong?

Sometimes we say He wanted darkness as a background, like the black velvet upon which a diamond is displayed, a clouded sky through which the sunshine bursts. After all, who will appreciate the light if there is no darkness? Who will appreciate acts of beauty and kindness if there are no deeds of ugliness and selfishness?

So the darkness is there for the sake of light. Evil exists so that good might also be. Pain exists to make room for healing.

But this could not be the entire answer.

Why? Because if it were the entire answer, all darkness would provide some hint of light, some glimmer of hope, some weakness by which it could be pierced.

But when He removed the light, the resulting darkness allowed not even a possibility of light. It was absolute, a void, an emptiness, the diametric opposite of the infinite light that preceded it—so that we find evil in our world that has no explanation, no answer, no light to shine.

The answer must be that darkness has a purpose and meaning of its own. That in light for the sake of light, G-d cannot be found. Because then He would be defined by the need to shine light, to create a world and to be present in that world. He would be defined by the act of being.

A time will come when the very darkness, otherness, coarseness of this physical existence will itself speak the most profound truths of its Creator.

The physical eye will see that which the mind cannot fathom. The pebbles beneath your feet will sing a divine song. And even all that which opposed you in your mission in life, that which is now ugly and nasty, that which mocks you and makes life a painful struggle—all of that will rush to assist you, to teach you, to reveal to you the deepest wisdom.

The most vital question still remains. Not a philosophical or a theological question, but one that concerns us here and now: How do we achieve this? How do we get the world to this point—that the darkness itself should speak out its truth?

We can flood the world with more and greater light, but that alone will not achieve the goal. Neither will raising the darkness to a place of greater light. No, we want that this darkness, here, as it is, to shine and speak its own truth.

And it does. Because it challenges us at every turn. It denies everything in which we believe—that there is purpose and meaning, that G-d is good and He is one. It laughs at our ambitions and scorns our enthusiasm, sets fire to our dreams, and pours buckets of ice upon our greatest aspirations.

And when it challenges us this way, we defy it, stubbornly, repeatedly, from the immovable essence-core of our souls. We show it that all its efforts are futile and vain, for we are bound up inextricably with the core of truth. And so we too are beyond darkness and light, self and not self, being and not being.

To which the darkness must eventually respond, "Yes. That is all I am here to say."

Darkness speaks, in silence. We will make it sing.

48

freedom out of darkness

Free choice is the quintessential expression of G-d, for He alone is truly free. G-d breathes within the human being, and so we, too, become free to choose our path home.

Darkness, confusion, and the possibility of evil—all this then has a purpose of its own: It provides a stage for us to find G-d within ourselves, seen only when we make the right choice, all on our own.

the choice

Ultimately, darkness will meet its end. Our choice lies only in the form of its demise:

If we meet nothing but success at every stage of our mission, darkness will helplessly surrender and deliver to our hand every spark of the divine it has so jealously held captive.

When we fail, however, we have taken upon ourselves to wrestle darkness face to face until its utter annihilation. Darkness will not surrender—no trace will be left of it that can do so. Darkness itself will have been transformed to light.

There is no greater light than when darkness shines.

faith in the dark

Do you only believe when you can see with your eyes? Is your faith only when your prayers are answered and miracles carry you on their wings?

Or do you also hold tight when circumstances fly in the face of all you believe to be true?

On the contrary, let the challenge take you to a place where your faith touches you to the core. There it is a belief you truly own. There it is as real to you as life itself. There it does not change.

And if it does not change, then you are bound up with the true essence of G-d, a G-d who does not change, and whose belief in you never ends.

51

light meets dark

Wherever light radiates, it does not find darkness. For light, darkness does not exist.

Wherever darkness spreads, it does not find light. For darkness, light does not exist.

In a time yet to come, the two shall meet and know one another in perfect union. At that nexus, we will see the One who created all things.

In the meantime, we glimpse a premonition of that wonder. For this is the human being: A breath of the divine within a material body; light and darkness face-to-face within a single being.

Balaam

Our greatest blessings were uttered not by Moses, not by David, not even by G-d Himself.

They were uttered by a wicked sorcerer, hired to curse.

The most brilliant diamonds hide in the deepest bowels of the earth;
the most intense blessings in the darkest caverns of life.

53

trickle of delight

Every moment that your soul inhabits this world, she can provide delight to her Maker above.

After 70, 80, maybe 120 years, your soul will ascend to a place above, a place of ecstasy as great as your soul can experience without dissolving into nothingness.

And what is that ecstasy?

No more than a trickle of the pleasure G-d has from the labor of your soul here, now.

54

squeezed by the barriers

They say nothing limits you other than your own imagination.

So you will say, "What, then, of the forces of nature? The constraints of a human body? Pain, exhaustion, and hunger? The hard reality I slam into whenever I attempt to stride through the barriers of life?"

Yes, they are there. But they are not barriers. Because they are not there to stop you. They are there to squeeze out the oil inside you.

Your soul pulls forward, and those barriers force her inward, towards her deepest, strongest self.

melting evil

Evil is darkness; nothing more than an absence of light.

It has no life of its own.

It is powered entirely by our fear of it, by our considering it a "something" that demands our response.

Evil is a terrorist, nursed on every spoonful of worry, encouraged with every glance of trepidation, fortified with every concession we make from our lives to acknowledge its threat—until it has soaked from us sufficient energy to rise brazenly and attack us with our own instruments.

So it is with the evil in the world, so it is with the destructive forces within each of us: When we stoop to conquer the evil within ourselves, we end up rolling with it in its mud.

To truly banish evil, you must march on the clouds and never look down. You must climb higher until you attain a place so filled with light there is no crevice left in which darkness may hide.

Lifted to that place, evil melts in surrender. For now it has fulfilled its purpose of being: To squeeze out the inner light of the human soul, a light that knows no bounds.

Mission accomplished, evil vanishes in the light it has called forth.

56

internal terrorism

Each of us has a terrorist inside, a mad impulse to abandon that which is rightfully ours, to blow ourselves to smithereens.

You cannot outsmart it, for it has hijacked the mind that you use. It believes it is you; you believe you are it.

No peace can be made with it, no compromise—for compromise is the name of its game, step by step to your oblivion.

You cannot even recognize its existence—for that would be your admission that evil has a place in G-d's world.

There is only one solution:

If you know what is right, do that.

Do not stop to look backwards—certainly not to negotiate with a terrorist.

57

conquest

Show a mighty emperor the world and ask him where he most desires to conquer.

He will spin the globe to the furthest peninsula of the most far-flung land, stab his finger upon it and declare, "This! When I have this, then I shall have greatness!"

In those places most finite, where the light of day barely trickles in, there the Infinite Light most yearns to be found.

mixtures

In this world there is no beauty without ugliness, no joy without sorrow, no pleasure without pain.

You cannot invent a thing that will provide benefit without threat of harm.
Neither is there a human on this earth who does only good without fault.

From the time we ate from the Tree of Knowing Good and Evil, our world became a place of compounds and mixtures.

Wherever you will find another form of good, you will find another sort of evil. Expel that evil, another will take its place. Rare it is, so rare, to find pure and simple goodness in a single being.

Therefore, do not reject any thing for the harm it may render, nor despise any man for the ugliness you find within him.

Rather, use each thing towards the purpose for which G-d conceived it, and learn from each man all the good he has to offer.

59

help from the past

All the souls of these generations have been here before. And they come with their baggage—both good and not so good.

But there is a distinction:

The good the soul has collected is eternal. It can never be uprooted, it can never fade away, for it is G-dly, and G-d does not change.

But the bad is not a thing of substance. It is an emptiness, a vacancy of light. As the soul makes her journey, through trials and travails, through growth and renewal, that darkness falls away, never to return.

Know yourself only as you are here in this life, and the challenges of our times are beyond perseverance.

Tap into the reservoir of your soul from the past, and find there the powers of millennia.

stop groping

Turn on the light.

Fine, blunder around in the dark, carefully avoiding every pit. Grope through the murky haze for the exit, stumbling and falling in the mud, then struggling back to your feet to try again.

But why not just turn on the light?

Lift yourself up, plug yourself in, immerse yourself in the wisdom of Torah, and ignite the love and joy within your heart.

Even if the light is ever so faint, it will be enough. For the weakest flame can push away the darkness of an enormous cavern.

61

rock bottom

At the peaks of life, you can catch a glimmer of the light of your soul.

When you hit rock bottom, you can touch its very core.

still rock bottom

Sometimes reaching higher is not enough. Sometimes you need to touch the very core of your soul. And there are two ways to do that:

One is by hitting rock bottom.

The other is by realizing that as high as you may have climbed, relative to where you really belong, this is still rock bottom.

the captive

*...the betrothed maiden screamed out, but there was
no one to save her*

—*Deuteronomy 22:27*

He does not want to be in that place. He feels himself a captive of
his own desires, now a prisoner incapable of escape. Deep within
him a voice screams—the scream of an innocent maiden under
assault, yet hopeless that anyone can save her.

On occasion, he breaks free of the clutches of his captor, perhaps
for a day, a week, maybe even an entire year—and then he is back
again, and all seems futile.

It is never futile. The One who made him knows the struggle he
fights. That brief victory, as fleeting as it may have been, is more
precious to his Creator than the deeds of the most righteous. A
precious soul has returned to Him, if even for a moment. And she
returned because the soul, at her essence, is only good.

If only he would know that delight of his Creator, nothing could
stop him. He would overcome all bounds and never fall back again.
Because his Creator's delight would become his delight, and the
two would bond in an inseparable bond.

For in truth, they were always so bonded, only now it is no longer
from afar.

G-d raw

If I wished to find all that is real and true at its very core, I would not find it in the ecstasy of the prayer of the devoted, nor in the epiphanies of the enlightened. I would not find it in the deeds of the righteous, nor in the love and kindness of those who live in harmony.

There, I would find a blinding light, an infinite light—but I would not find G-d Himself.

If I wished to find G-d as He is at His essence, beyond all light and darkness, beyond the infinite and the boundless, I would come to the place of those who struggle daily to escape their muck and mire, those who labor to pierce the wall of their prison so that even a glimmer of light could break through, and even as they fail, try again and again.

For this struggle, all light was created. To the aid of this struggle, G-d Himself descends. When those walls are pierced, the Creator exclaims, "It was worth it, all this creation! It was worth it for this alone!"

65

a duel of beasts

The rabbis of the Talmud, who lived in Roman times, taught that in a time yet to come, G-d will entertain us with a duel of wild beasts, much as would entertain the vulgar mobs in their coliseums.

We will watch and we will cheer on the victor. We will gasp as he falls and rejoice as he picks himself up again to continue the battle.

And we will realize that this victor is each one of us, as we were fighting against the darkness in which we were cast as we lived within this world.

Then we will laugh an unbridled laugh. Then we will know the unbounded delight of our Creator as He watched our victory, here in this world now.

duets

On the other side of ecstasy lies a painful emptiness.
On the other side of bitterness lies joy.

Where one goes, the other must follow.

In the ecstasy of understanding lies the gnawing pain of
a new frontier of ignorance.

In the agony of yearning lies the ecstasy of love.

In the ecstasy of prayer lies the agony of smallness and
distance before the infinite light.

There is no sweet song that is not equally bitter, save
that which is shallow and meaningless.

He formed His world from delight and so must share in
its bitterness.

Until the time when the bitter will be sweet, when
darkness will shine.

67

lifted by the past

When do you know that you have truly returned and changed your past?

As long as that past keeps pulling you down, it remains what it always was.

When that past drives you higher and yet higher each day, then you know that the past has been transformed.

return with love

Don't waste a good sin.

"All that G-d does is good, even the wicked person on the day of his wickedness."—Proverbs 16:4

Why did a G-d who hates evil create a world where evil can take charge of a human being? Only so that this human being would be driven yet higher than could ever be reached without sin.

Return out of fear, and the sin has not accomplished its goal. It is a wasted sin.

Return out of love, and the night has found its day. It has driven you higher.

life lives on

Why is there death in the world?
So that evil will not live forever.

Because, since we ate of the Tree of Knowledge, no one
walks forward without stumbling, no one climbs without
falling, no one does good all his life without causing
some damage along the way.

Until, at the end, our lives are an absurd muddle of good
and evil, inextricably bound.

With death, evil dies as well. The failures, the ugly acts,
even the damage done—all these wither and eventually
perish.

But the good we have accomplished—and that we truly
are—this lives forever.

preconception

Standing at the cusp of existence, before its very conception, when anything could have been, but nothing was; He declared, "It should be light."

The truth of all darkness is its mandate to become light; the truth of all conscious beings is their mandate to perceive that light; the truth of all existence is to know that it emerges out of that which stands beyond existence.

"How great are Your works, O G-d! How very deep are Your thoughts!"—Psalms 92:6

the bottomless pit

In this life, to climb yet higher you will always need to first descend.

Often, in the descent, the mountain can be seen from afar.

But sometimes, all you see is a bottomless pit.

It's those descents that take you higher than any eye can perceive.

light's advantage

There was darkness and there was light. And He chose light.

He didn't have to choose light. He could have chosen an eternal wrestling match of light and dark. What greater pleasure can there be than the aroma of darkness struck down and transformed to a throne for light?

Nevertheless, he chose light. He chose to set a time for the obliteration of darkness, a time of pure and perfect light. And what does He have from that?

He needs nothing from that. That is the plan He so desired.

song and silence

Each thing sings. And each is silent.

Each thing sings, pulsating with the life G-d gives it.

And each is silent. And the silence speaks, saying, "I am. I am just a thing that is."

The silence is also G-d.

For He is the only one who can truly say, "I just am."

poor reception

Evil does not descend from above. The transmission from above is pure and coherent. Evil is distortion and noise, an artifact of our reception.

If we would only adjust our reception devices, our attitude and our ability to receive, the signal would become clear.

And that is all of life—adjusting reception.

75

deep roots

There are times when our eyes are closed, our minds can only dream aimlessly, and our hearts are as lifeless, impervious stone. And yet we stand firm, with stubborn chutzpah, us against an entire world.

The mind and the heart have their roots. But that stubborn chutzpah, that knowledge of who you are and what is the truth for which you stand, its roots reach to a source of living waters that never cease nor change.

the lost ark

In Solomon's Temple, there were two places reserved for the Holy Ark: One in the Holy of Holies, and one hidden deep beneath that chamber.

There are two places to find G-d's presence in all its glory.

One is in the most holy of chambers, beyond the place of light and heavenly incense. There, G-d Himself could be found by the most perfect of mortals on the most sublime day of the year.

Today, we cannot enter that place. But there is another place, a place always accessible, beyond catacombs and convoluted mazes, deep within the earth's bowels.

There, those whose faces are charred with the ashes of failure, their hands bloody from scraping through dirt and stone, their clothes torn from falling again and again, and their hearts ripped by bitter tears, there, in that subterranean darkness, they are blinded by the light of the hidden things of G-d...

...until that Presence will shine for all of us, forever.

close & dark

When does the moon have no light for us?
When it is closest to the sun.

The closer it comes to alignment between
us and the sun, the more it diminishes in
size. Until, at its closest point, it altogether
disappears. Then, once again, it is renewed and
begins to shine.

At those points in life when we peer into
darkness, groping for some clue why this is
happening to us, where this is taking us, why
we must go through all this—those are the
points of closeness to the light, the points of
renewal.

demand your rights

We have the right to demand that the Moshiach should arrive now despite our failures.

We have the right and the obligation to demand a redemption without travail, a birth without pain.

We have already stared darkness in its face; we have marched through its tunnel in a holocaust across the sea. We have passed enough tests. We have polished enough dark buttons until they glisten brightly.

All that is left is for us to demand that which is due. Long due.

That, after all, is the *halachah*: A workman is not due his pay until he submits his bill.

meaning

What is the meaning?
  The meaning is a story.
A story told before there was any time in which a story could
occur:
  Your soul,
a pure child of G-d,
a fractal of the very essence of wisdom,
a breath of life from the innermost source of life,
  will descend from her place,
lower and yet lower,
to clothe herself in a body,
blood and sinews driven by a beast within,
and she will tie her destiny to theirs...
  ...and this body,
along with whatever maddening beast drives that body,

and the entire world in which this soul will dwell,
will do all they can to conceal and negate the light of that divine
soul...

...and yet, despite every challenge,
this soul of yours will purify and elevate that body and its beast,
as well as the share of this world to which she has been assigned.

G-d Himself will celebrate in great delight.

Why?

Because the One who transcends all bounds desires to be found
in all His essence within our tightly bounded world.

And that will come through us, struggling here with the restrictions and challenges of our world.

And what is the reason He so desires?

There is no reason.

If there were a reason, you would ask, "What is the reason for the
reason?"

But this is the desire where all begins.

It is a desire that transcends reason;
it is the place from which all reason is born.

And so it is unbounded and all-consuming.

For it is not a desire of a human being.

It is not a desire of one who has limited will—or of any being or
entity at all.

It is a desire that lies at the very core of all being.

That core of being chose to desire,
and now there is nothing else.

G-d in action

G-d is better grasped in actions than in ideas.

inside workers

When you look at a human being, you see his hands working, his feet walking, his mouth talking. You don't see his heart, his brain, his lungs and kidneys. They work quietly, inside. But they are the essential organs of life.

The world, too, has hands and feet—those who are making the news, moving things around, shaking things up.

The heart, the inner organs, they are those who work quietly from the inside, unnoticed. Those who speak with the Creator from deep within, those who bring the light of Torah into the world, those who do a simple act of kindness with no thought of reward.

81

beyond sincerity

Sincerity is not enough. You have to do the right thing. You might be truly sincere about your generosity and your *mitzvot*, but if it doesn't reach the right place, or was not done the right way, it still did not succeed.

Why is it this way? Why can't we be judged by our intentions alone?

So we will know that we are small, and Truth is very large. It is Truth that stands at the center, and we who orbit about it.

the quantum
leap

There are times when moving forward step by step is not enough. There are times when you can't just change what you do, how you speak, and how you think about things.

Sometimes, you need to pick up both feet off the ground and leap.

Sometimes, you need to change at your very core of being.

being paradox

*And the Israelites walked on the dry land within
the sea, and the water was a wall for them to
their right and to their left.*

—Exodus 14:29

Always be leaving the slavery of Egypt. Never say, "I am this."

If you catch yourself fitting into a definition, contradict it.
If you have found your comfort zone, go beyond it. Don't let
anything define you—neither to the left, nor to the right.

All single roads lead back to bondage. Only by walking two
opposite roads at once can you be free.

Yes, it demands a miracle. So be it. Always be walking through
the splitting of the sea.

both ways

One who loves must learn fear. One who fears must learn love.

The thinker must do. The doer must think.

The pacifist must fight, the fighter must find peace.

If you flow as a river, burn as a fire. If you burn as a furnace, flow as a river. If you fly as a bird, sit firm as a rock. If you sit firmly, then fly as a bird.

Be a fire that flows; a rock that flies. Love with fear and fear with love.

For we are not fire, nor water, nor air, nor rocks, nor thoughts, nor deeds, nor fear, nor love.

We are divine beings.

85

within beyond

Be as the Infinite Light:

Be within, stay above.

be real

What is your job in this world? It is to be real.

Act real, mean what you say, think and really be thinking, talk to your Creator and let the words flow from your heart. Every cell of your body down to your fingernails should be real.

Yes, everyone knows there are so many things to accomplish in life and everyone agrees it's better if they're done with sincerity.

That's not what is meant. This is what you're here to accomplish—to be real.

go to yourself

Go to yourself...to the land that I will show you.
—Genesis 12:1

There, in the land, I will show you your own essence.
—Torah Or, Lech Lecha 11b

The spiritual world of meditation and prayer has its borders:
    That which can be known will be known.
    That which is beyond knowing is permitted to whisper, softly.
    And the very core of your being cannot utter a word of its
presence.

But when the soul descends into the world of action,
then every rule can be broken,
every boundary crossed.

So G-d says to Abraham and to us, his children:
    Take your soul out into the world, take her very essence there.
    Find divine purpose in your work;
    discover G-d within the commonplace workings of this
    everyday world.

You will come to know that which cannot be known.
Your soul will see that which she could never lay bare—
    her very core of being.

In this world, the soul knows no borders.

better than the sun

There are three approaches to dealing with this world:

One is to remain aloof as the sun. The world will benefit from your light, but you will remain distant and removed. You will invest little in this world and so have little to lose.

Another approach is to wane and wax as the moon—to suffer the scars and bruises of life, delight in its offerings, thirst for its rewards, and tremble at its horrors—to invest everything and risk losing it all.

Or you can be both the sun and the moon at once. You can feel meaning and purpose in every episode of life, no matter how small. And, at the same time, remain above it all.

What is the secret? It is memory.

Even as you throw yourself into this world, remember you are not the body, but the soul.

89

don't just stand there

As long as you're holding on to where you were yesterday, you're standing still.

seasons of essence

There is the body, the soul, and then there is the essence.

If the soul is light, then the essence is the source of light. If the soul is energy, then the essence is her generator. It is not something you have. It is who and what you are.

Most of our lives, as hard as we might try, we can only dance around that essence-core, unable to enter within. We meditate, we pray, we are inspired—but to touch our inner core, the place from whence all this comes, it takes a power from beyond.

That is why there are seasons in life empowered from beyond. Special days and special nights, times of crisis and times of joy that touch the core. At other times you can step forward. At those times, you can leap into a new form of being.

91

the freedom connection

We are limited by the very fact that we have human form. There is no freedom in following our whim or instinct, only slavery. Even our most reasoned decisions are ultimately subjective. As a prisoner cannot undo his own shackles, so we remain enslaved to our own limited selves.

Therefore, Moses was told, "When you take the people out of Egypt, you shall all serve the Infinite G-d on this mountain."

The Infinite G-d is the only one who is not compelled by any bounds. What makes us free? Simple deeds done each day, as agents of the One who is absolutely free.

no repeats

If you are serving the same G-d today as you served yesterday, what kind of god have you made for yourself?

Can G-d be frozen and defined? Does He get older with each day? Does He eventually, then, become of a relic of the past?

Where there is love and where there is awe, each day brings a new discovery of wonder.

pressurized escape

Your soul, before she came here below, stepped higher and higher each day.

So why did she descend below? What did she gain by coming here?

Because when you have the power of the infinite, stepping higher each day is standing still. It is a prison of "being that."

Unchallenged, the soul knows no better. She must descend below, and here, within the ultimate confines, she will learn to leap, to break out of all boundaries, to escape the prison of being. To be "not that."

94

prison

Torah has no concept of prison as a punishment. Why? Because prison is a futile place. A place where you are told, "You must be in this place, but you must not change what this place is. You will grow older, but you must not take charge of your life. You will live, but you must not give life."

A living human being must effect change in his world, must take charge of his life, must give life to others.

Just as no one can give without receiving, so, too, no one can receive without giving.

95

prison juice

There are times when G-d will put a soul in prison—often a very lofty soul, such as Joseph. Not as a punishment, but as a cocoon, a bridge to an entirely new state of being.

It is like being held in a vise. Squeezed with the ultimate of futility, the deepest powers of the soul break through, for this soul and for all those who are bound up with this soul.

96

the invisible prison

The ultimate prison is when G-d locks you up. He doesn't need guards or cells or stone walls. He simply decides that, at this point in life, although you have talent, you will not find a way to express it. Although you have wisdom, there is nobody who will listen. Although you have a soul, there is nowhere for her to shine.

And you scream, "Is this why You sent a soul into this world? For such futility?"

That is when He gets the tastiest, essence of your juice squeezed out of you.

seeding
miracles

The soil of the earth was imbued with a wondrous power—the power to generate life. Place a tiny seed in the ground, and it will convert the carbon of the air into a mighty redwood.

Yet another miracle, even more wondrous: A quiet act of kindness buried so that no one will see ignites an explosion of divine light.

Infinite power is hidden in the humblest of places.

a small
candle

You don't need to move mountains. You just have to know where to aim.

You can transform an entire family forever just with one candle lit by one little girl.

G-d with the oppressed

*G-d is always with the oppressed. Even if the oppressor is
righteous and the oppressed is wicked, our Sages tell us,
G-d is with the oppressed.*

—*Vayikra Rabbah 27:7*

Visit the prisoners and bring them some happiness. Even if they are
guilty, even if, in your eyes, they deserve whatever misery they have.
Bring them joy.

the parable

The world is a parable, two stories at once;
one layered beneath the other.

On the outside, it is the story of a brute
called Reality, a bloodless monster hosting
an army of fiends, beasts, lunacy, and,
worst of all, futility.

On the inside, it is a story of its own
Author with you alone, in eternal love,
and every challenge of this adventure just
another expression of that love, drawing
the two of you yet closer.

The world is a parable, a story on two
channels at once.
On which channel do you choose to spend
your precious time?

101

the river up

When the divine light began its awesome descent—a journey to create one world and then a lower world, and yet a lower world, for endless worlds, condensing and compacting infinite power into finite packages, until focused to the fine, crystallized resolution of the nature of this world—it did so with purpose: to bring forth a world of continuous ascent.

Since that beginning, not a day has passed that does not transcend its yesterday.

Like a mighty river rushing to reach its ocean, no dam can hold it back, no creature can struggle against its current. If we appear to fall backward, to take a wrong turn, to lose a day in failure—it is only an illusion, for we have no map to know its way. We see from within, but the river knows its path from above. And to that place above all is drawn.

We are not masters of that river— not of our ultimate destiny, nor of the stops along the way, not even of the direction of our travel. We did not create the river—its flow creates us. It is the blood and soul of our world, its pulse and its warmth.

Yet of one thing we have been given mastery: Not of the journey, but of our role within it.

How soon will we arrive? How complete? How fulfilled? Will we be the spectators? Or simply the props?

Or will we be the heroes?

G-d's question

Before He brought the cosmos into being, all that now exists was no more than a question in His mind, a counterpoint of ideas, pondering, "Should it be? Or should it not?"

Then, from that thought, He created all things, and out of all things He formed Adam.

"And He breathed into his nostrils the breath of life, and Adam became a living being."

So Adam awoke and he began to ponder: Is there really a world? Should there be a world? Why should there be anything at all? Is it worthwhile?

And now that is the struggle within each of us.

103

leading forward

You do not need to attain perfection in order to lead.

You need only to discover which way is forward and begin moving in that direction.

104

mission impossible

We were not placed here to do the possible, to bring cause into effect, potential into actual. G-d does not breathe His spirit within us so that we should achieve the facile and the ordinary.

We are here to achieve the impossible. To teach the world tricks it feigns it cannot do. To fill it with light it does not know. To make the blind see, the deaf hear, the bitter sweet, the darkness shine. To make everyday business into mystic union. To rip away the façade of the world and to bring it to confess its secret oneness with the Divine.

When they tell you, "You can't go on that path, it's beyond you!" grab that path as your destiny.

105

power of one

One individual brought the world to the brink of destruction—if not for the mercies of the Master of the Universe, who ordained, "The earth shall stand firm and not fall."

Such is the power of a single human being to do evil.

A thousand times over is the power of each one of us to do good.

106

hyper-faith

We are more than believers.
      We are believers in believing.

We know its power
      and have perfect faith it will work.

a light for 100

A dish of food fills one stomach, but the next in line is still hungry.

Even the warmth of a furnace must be turned higher if more freezing souls appear.

But a light that guides one person will guide a hundred.

Be that light.

the now

Once upon a time, there was a world that was a place of magnificence, awe, and beauty. We, as sentient beings, were privy to a small glimpse of that beauty. Even to grasp some of the wisdom that stood behind it.

And that is how we explained many things—as glimpses of a higher beauty.

Then we began to measure everything. Ingeniously. We measured the swinging of a pendulum. We measured the speed of falling objects. By counting and measuring, we found we could predict and invent. We found that when we spoke of quantities, we were far more accurate than our predecessors, who spoke in terms of the qualities of things.

We found ways to apply algebra to the dimensions of objects. And then to the motion of objects—in the form of calculus. Rapidly, the universe began to divulge secrets we had never imagined. And rapidly, it became a very different universe. A world of numbers and things that could be counted with numbers.

As for beauty, magnificence, and all the rest—all those things that elude measurement—eventually they became the subjective realm of the human mind alone. Today, to some, they are mere illusions, epiphenomena somehow related to survival mechanisms in ways not yet fully understood.

This new paradigm has proven invaluable. But it wears no clothes. You can live without clothes; a paradigm is a paradigm even if it is incomplete. But don't delude yourself that you have answered any questions when you have done so only by creating a much greater one.

How is it that out of a cold, mechanical universe emerges a warm, sentient being that feels, knows, is conscious, and stands in awe before its beauty—a beauty that exists only as a figment of the gray matter in its skull?

Isn't this the height of human audacity—to assume that we are fantastic instances of consciousness that have somehow emerged out of a dumb universe? Isn't this much like the teenager who can't understand how such a bright guy like him came from parents who have no brains?

How did we come to such a bizarre delusion? Werner Heisenberg wrote, "In classical physics, science started from the belief—or should one say, from the illusion?—that we could describe the world, or at least parts of the world, without any reference to ourselves."

Heisenberg again: "What we observe is not nature itself, but nature exposed to our method of questioning." For 500 years, our questions have been with a caliper, a clock, and Cartesian coordinates. Have we forgotten how to question with a raw sense of mind and being?

Thomas Kuhn called the transition from qualities to quantification the great paradigm shift. But, in truth, was there ever a need to reject the original paradigm? Simply because the universe lends itself to measurement does that imply it is made of numbers? Simply because we cannot apply our science to that which cannot be measured, does that imply that all things can be measured, and that all that counts can be counted?

Perhaps it is all a single paradigm. Perhaps the world is a place of beauty, passion, wisdom and consciousness, desire and delight—and those are its true being, its very soul—and yet all these manifest themselves in forms that can be measured.

And if you should ask: But if beauty is a thing that cannot be measured, then how is it that we can measure, weigh, calculate, and predict its glimmer? Where does the magic happen that quality is transformed into quantities?

For this, there is a simple retort: If the human mind is capable of transporting its perceptions of measurable, tangible objects on a journey to become things of awe and wonder, why should the reverse not also be possible—that awe and wonder should make their journey to appear in our world of tangible perception?

We ourselves are an analogy for such a universe: We dream, we love, we fear, and we ponder. And then we express those inner feelings as outward expressions. Because I see you smile, does that mean there is nothing more to happiness than a muscular reaction of facial muscles?

And perhaps the most wondrous thing about this world is that it allows us to measure, predict, and know anything at all. That we can perceive its smile.

Indeed, this is precisely what mathematics is about—the power of metaphor, the wondrous capacity we have to perceive reality from multiple perspectives on multiple planes. With mathematics, we are able to represent three—even four or more—dimensions on a two-dimensional plane, or even in the form of symbols on a page. But does that imply that there really are no dimensions, only symbols?

Wave-frequencies and durations are not music. The letters on a page are not the story of a book. So, too, all our numbers and calculations, as ingenious and useful as they may be, are not the universe itself.

And the proof—if I had all of them on my computer, I would still not have a universe. There is music, there is a story. There is a world.

This is also the secret of all art—the skill of the artist to squeeze his entire soul into the rules and disciplines of his art. The story-teller develops consistent, believable characters. The composer constricts his music to the rules of harmony and counterpoint. The artist determines his palette. The author knows well the rules and constructs of his language.

Art is as much about constriction as it is about expression. You could even say that art is the act of quantifying beauty. And in that way, we, the created being, emulate our Creator as He expresses His own infinite, unknowable beauty in the tightly bounded and measurable terms of a real world.

When we marry the two paradigms, a new concept of our world emerges.

Within the first paradigm, the true world is the world of perfect forms and qualities, a world beyond and above. Ours is a deep, dark cavern, with a crack here and there through which some distorted reflection of a reflection of that true light occasionally trickles in. It is a world to escape.

Within the second paradigm, there is nothing above. Beauty is a figment of the mind. All that is of value, then, is that which exists in our minds. It is a world to exploit.

When the two paradigms are seen as two facets of a single truth, everything changes. Our world is of inherent value. It is the ultimate expression of the divine. It is the ultimate work of art, and we are its players, its audience, and its privileged caretakers.

The great oceans, the forests, the virtually endless diversity of creatures of land, sky, and sea—all are strokes lifted from a divine palette of beauty and magnificence.

The compassion of one human being for another, the wisdom gained from each day upon this earth, the cycle of giving life and watching that life give life—in these we know that which transcends knowing.

And how wondrous, how precious, how divine, the story of our own people, their endurance, the beauty of their deeds, and their oneness that cannot be found anywhere else in the world. In our story and in our deeds—and in the endless wisdom of Torah that sustains that story and counsels those deeds—there we touch and merge with G-d Himself, in a union that could not be had in any ethereal world.

As it stands on its own, the world is a nothingness. As a work of art, it is the ultimate expression of the beauty of its Creator. And of what value is beauty if there is no art?

In the Jewish tradition, this inner depth of magnificence, awesomeness, beauty, of wisdom, ingenuity and delight—these are called the divine sefirot. They are the modalities by which the Creator has chosen to express Himself in His world, and by which His creatures are capable of reaching out to their Creator.

The character of the human being is composed of a microform of those sefirot—in the words of the Maggid of Mezritch, "As silent ashes are to a living tree." They resonate as our sense of consciousness, our appreciation of beauty, and our capacity to make sense of the universe in which we dwell.

The articulations, the strokes of beauty within each thing, those are the divine sparks, the force of life that sustains the very existence of each creature and endows it with its particular nature.

Our role is to discover, to embrace, to cherish those sparks, and to reconstruct them into a complete whole. Our Torah is our guide, and our goal is the messianic times, closely upon us.

That would be a wonderful place to end. But it would lack integrity. The materialists, after all, deserve a better answer to a hard question: How is it that an abstraction such as beauty can be measured and handled in a world so tangible as ours?

Yes, we answered that. We said that is the power of metaphor. And all our world is a metaphor—just as is mathematics and art.

But the key to art is not simply to create. The artist must remove himself from his work, allowing it to be born into its own life.

And there is a crucial difference between the means by which we remove ourselves from our work and allow it to become real, and the way our world emerges into being.

The artist is capable of removing himself because he is not the creator of the resources that he chooses. We mold clay or silver, breathe sound into a flute, or mix and match the elements of human personality to contrive characters for our story. We shape that which is already there.

In the act of creating a universe from nothing, there are no such resources to work from. Beauty itself must descend and crystalize into forms that can be touched and measured. And its Creator must be present within it at every moment, while concealing that presence at the same moment.

In the case of our world, not only the form and life of each being must be constantly streamed, but the very substance of each object, its time and space, and even its sense that it exists.

Which means that we are not mere projections of light. We, and everything in our world, are crystallizations of the creative force itself. That force is here, within each thing. It is being whatever that thing is—while at the same moment remaining entirely transcendent and concealed, so as to allow each being a sense that it truly exists.

And at the same time, nothing has ever left its origin. We sense our autonomy, our ego, our life of our own—and yet even that is nothing more than an articulation of our Creator's desire. He desires a world that is truly a world.

Which is another way of saying that G-d is here now, while at the same time, entirely beyond. As the *Zohar* states, "You are He who grasps all things, and yet none of them can grasp You."

The quantum fields that hold matter in its patterns of expansion and contraction, the trajectories of electrons and the vibrations of the most fundamental elements of our world—all are consistently sustained by a creative force, streaming forth from a higher wisdom. As are the flowering of a blossom, the bubbling of a brook, the mitosis of cells, and the eruption of supernovae.

The energy of being flows continuously from the Source of Being, condensing and concealing itself within itself, again and again for uncountable agains, until ultimately crystallizing as our material reality—yet, all the time remaining a nothingness, as a ray of light within an infinite source of light, as a single articulation of being within a free and boundless Absolute Being.

So that if for a moment that current would cease, all of existence would cease with it. There would be no matter, no laws of physics, no fields of energy, no dimensions of space. Not only would all these be gone, they would never have been—time itself would be erased. For they are nothing more than articulations of a higher will, and if for a moment there were no will that they should be, they never were.

And if the current would begin again, in some different way than it was before, then the world would be a new world, and the past would be a new past.

Which means that the past, the present, and the future, all begin now.

No, we are not the authors of our world, nor the artists of this masterpiece. We are goats thrashing about in a rose-garden. Only that we are sentient goats, who should know better.

Yet, without an audience, there is no art. And art is only created for the sake of an audience. If so, it is an interactive performance of sorts, piercing the fourth wall, so that performer and audience become one.

That is the teaching of all the great masters of Kabbalah—that in this great work of purpose and meaning, we are vital players. Nothing can happen without us. And all that does happen depends on our deeds, here, in this world, now.

As Yehuda Moscato described us, we are the soloist of a grand concerto. As we play our part, so will the entire cosmos respond, whether in dissonance, or in harmony.

The Mishnah teaches, "Know that which is above you."

The Maggid of Mezritch read it is, "Know that all that occurs above comes from you."

His pupil, Rabbi Schneur Zalman of Liadi, read it as, "Know that all that exists above exists from you."

And the Rebbe explained, "Know that all of time, from the very first emergence of existence until the end of time, begins with you, now. Because according to whatever you will do now, so is determined all that ever was, is, and will be."

Each one of us sits at the vortex of magnificence. Everything depends on this moment now.

———◆———

108

come of days

And Abraham was aged, having entered into days.
—Genesis 24:1

Abraham, we are told, did not just age, but "entered into days." Meaning, he had brought all of himself into every one of his days.

Within each moment of life, whatever it was he needed to do, he invested his entire being.

And so he owned every day of his life. His life was his.

109

counting time

We count time as though it were money. But in what way is it so?

We can make more money, but we can't make more time.

Money can vanish in multiple ways, but time can neither be stolen nor lost.

Every penny of our money can be spent or saved, invested or loaned, but time—the hours slip through our fingers, allowing us not the slightest mastery over their incessant stream.

Yet time relies upon us to count its moments.

Because if a moment enters and is wasted, it has come and gone without meaning. And without meaning, in what way did it exist?

A coin uncounted is a wasted coin. A moment uncounted is a moment that never was.

110

life in a day

Before you were formed in the womb, your days were numbered and set in place. They are the chapters of the lessons you came here to learn, the faces of the wisdom this world has to teach you, the gateways to the treasures this lifetime alone can bestow.

A day enters, opens its doors, tells its story, and then returns above, never to visit again. Never. For no two days of your life will share the same wisdom.

a year in a day

As the entirety of the sun is reflected in every glistening droplet of water, so is the entirety of time—every event that ever occurred, every creation that ever came into being, every life that ever lived, every battle ever fought, every desire, every love, every thought, every drama that was, is or is yet to be—reflected in the single droplet of time that is your life.

Not only is this grand story of the universe reflected in your lifetime, but in any single year of your life as well. For a year, in Hebrew, means **change**—a perfect droplet reflecting all the changes and seasons that ever were and ever will be.

And, in truth, every day is a droplet of life. For each and every day you are born, you live your life through, and you pass on from this world.

As it is for the the very smallest droplet of time, the droplet of this moment now: At every moment the entire universe is reborn, sings its entire song of past, present and future, and then returns to the void. Each moment is another world.

So that, yes, each day has its particular meaning and mission. But each day is also everything. As is every moment.

arrows of life

The life of Sarah was one hundred years and twenty years and seven years, the years of the life of Sarah
                                        —*Genesis 23:1*

All of them were equally good.
                                        —*Rashi*

In which direction does your life move? To wherever you have pointed its arrow.

If the arrow points forever backward, to blame the present on the past and to script the future accordingly, then what is to make life worth its pain, the story worth its struggle?

But if the arrow points forward to an unfolding destiny, then every pain becomes the cracking of a shell, every travail the shedding of a cocoon; as an olive releasing its oil to the press, a seedling breaking its path through rock and soil to reach the sun. What is the pain relative to the promise it holds?

Therefore, Sarah looked back after 127 years, and all her days, even the darkest, the weariest, were good and filled with beauty.

living time

People talk about "wasting time," or even "killing time."

Neither term is accurate. Time is not yours that you should waste it. Neither does it have a life of its own that you should take that away.

Rather, time awaits you to give it life.

114

untraditional life

We need tradition. Tradition preserves life, but it does not give life.

We need goals. Goals inspire life, but they are not life.

Life is here and now. To be alive, your here-and-now must touch the essence of your soul. To be alive, every moment must be a new life.

Therefore, our Sages said, "Every day the Torah must be new to you."

For if it is not new, then it is not your life. And if it is not your life, then what is?

115

balance

In a rush, in confusion, no one can serve his purpose upon this earth.

A life of purpose is a delicate balancing act of body and soul, heaven and earth. It requires two feet firmly upon the ground and a clear head high up in the air.

Only then are you the master.

In a rush, you are not in control of your world—the world is in control of you. Place your foot gently on the brakes, slow down, switch gears from madness to mind.

Reclaim mastery.

116

fire burning fire

Life is fire. We are beings of flames. Mostly, we burn with anxiety, with the angst of survival in a hostile world.

But we can harness our own fire: We can stop, contemplate, meditate, and pray. With these, we fan a different fire, a fire of love for the Infinite Light that lies beyond this world and encompasses all things.

One fire swallows another and we are set free. Liberated from fear, we face the world no longer as slaves, but as masters.

117

four gates

Judges and officers shall you appoint in all your cities....
—*Deuteronomy 16:18*

Think of yourself as a city. You have four magical gates: The Gate of Seeing, the Gate of Listening, the Gate of Imagining, and the Gate of Speaking.

Magical gates, because an Infinite G-d enters your finite city through these gates. An Infinite G-d who cannot be squeezed within any place or boxed within any definition, but chooses to dress neatly in a wisdom called Torah—and these are your gates by which wisdom may enter.

That is why all the world competes to storm those gates. They want you to see the ugliness they see, hear the cacophony they hear, imagine the nonsense they imagine, and speak without end. And then, you will desire all they desire, and no room will be left in your city for that Infinite G-d.

You only need to master those gates and the city is yours.

118

live clothing

We wear a suit that has a life of its own.

It is knitted of the fabric of words, images, and sounds, mischievous characters that no one else can see—or would care to know.

You, however, hear them day and night, chattering, buzzing, playing their games in the courtyard of your mind. They are the threads and the fabric of the garment of thought that envelopes you.

Leave your thoughts to play on their own, and this garment will take you for a walk to places you never wanted to see.

Grab the controls, master this suit. Provide a script, direct your thoughts—those characters will play along.

Do something quick, because you, after all, are dressed up within them.

119

keep the windows open

Our souls are the windows through which the world is filled with light, pores through which it breathes, channels to its supernal source.
There is no function more vital to our universe, nothing more essential to its fulfillment, since for this it was formed.

When we do acts of love, speak words of kindness, and teach wisdom, those windows open wide.
When we fail, those windows cloud over and shut tight.

It is such a shame, this loss of light, this lost breath of fresh air. A stain can be washed away, but a moment of life, how can it be returned?

panic

Panic, confusion, and pessimism, these are the nightmares of a heart freely handed the reins to your mind.

Reverse the process. Hand your mind the reins to your heart.

Feed yourself with wholesome thoughts. With all your willpower, stay focused on those thoughts. Ignore the burning panic in your heart; refuse to allow it to distract you.

Soon enough, the black horse of pessimism gallops off into the night.

G-d's image

We were created in G-d's image. What is G-d's image? It is a vision. A vision that triggered the beginning of time.

From a point before and beyond all things, G-d looked upon a moment in time to be. He saw there a soul, distant from Him in a turbulent world, yet yearning to return to Him and His Oneness. And He saw the pleasure He would have from this reunion.

So He invested His infinite light into that finite image and became one with that image, and in that image He created each one of us.

That vision that He saw, was the current moment.

when is G-d?

G-d is found at two poles of time:

He is found outside of time.
And He is found here within the current moment.

From that point beyond time, G-d looks within the current moment, and says, "From this, I will have delight."

With that choice, all of past and future is created anew.

123

original success

Before your soul descended to this world, she was
destined to succeed. If not in this lifetime, then in
another, or yet another—eventually she will fulfill
her entire mission. And in each lifetime, she will
move further ahead.

It was this knowledge that conceived her.
It was this inspiration that brought the world to be.
It is this vision of her success that lies at the
essence of all things.

124

crossroads

There are crossroads where you choose not only your future, but your past as well.

Take one road, and your past becomes but an irrelevant and forgotten dream.

Take another road, and even the darkest past can become a magnificent frame for a moment of glory. The moment for which your soul was formed and all the past was made.

125

first day

All is defined by destiny. Even the past
is redefined by the arrow of its future.
The very existence of that time that held
that past is recreated once it achieves its
hidden destiny. A destiny that only you
can reveal.

That is all that matters: Now, the first day
of all of time—future and past.

126

happy birthday, universe

Every year, our Sages taught, with the cry of the shofar, the entire universe is reborn.

At that time, with our resolutions and our prayers, we hold an awesome power: To determine what sort of child this newborn year shall be—how it will take its first breaths, how it will struggle to its feet, and how it will carry us through life for the twelve months to come.

In truth, it is not only once a year: At every new moon, in a smaller way, all life is renewed again.

So, too, every morning, we are all reborn from a nighttime taste of death.

And at every moment—in the smallest increment of time—every particle of the universe is projected into being out of absolute nothingness, as it was at the very beginning.

Which is why there is always hope. Because at every moment, life is born anew. And we are the masters of how this moment will be born.

127

time travel

To change the past, there is no need to travel in a time machine. Everything can be done by remote control.

Here's how it works: From beyond the continuum of time, its Creator looks at where your spaceship is heading right now. From that point, He creates all its trajectory—through the future and through the past.

Switch the direction your past is sending you. Soon enough, it becomes a different past.

128

two channels

There are two channels on life's tv. On one plays a fantasy; the other is real life.

The fantasy is a world that imagines itself to be its own truth; where nothing is of intrinsic value, and everything functions by the rules of chance and necessity.

In this world, you are nothing more than another background or shadow, an extra in a plotless movie, a disposable prop for a five-second set.

In this world, life may be prosperous. Or disastrous. Whatever the scene demands, so you shall be given. Until it is time for the next scene to begin.

The real life is a world in which you stand face to face before the Director of this grand drama. But your story is not this drama. It is this intimate relationship of yours with the Director.

All things may change—the props, the backgrounds, the actors, even the play itself—but this is forever. It is truth.

129

heaven desires earth

There are those who chase all things of heaven—and find they cannot live.

There are those who chase all things of earth. Their life is not worth living.

Heaven desires the earth, and the earth is lost without heaven. Make your life a marriage of the two, as lovers that never part, and you will find peace.

130

beyond wisdom

Do not be misled by those who claim there is no purpose.

They may know life, but not its womb.

They may know darkness, but not its meaning.

They may have wisdom, but they cannot reach higher, to a place beyond wisdom,
a place from which all wisdom began.

They may reach so high until the very source from which all rivers flow.
To the place where all known things converge, where all knowledge is one.

But they have not touched the very core of being, the place before being begins, where it is chosen that being will begin, where there is nothing—no light, no darkness, no knowledge, no convergence, no wisdom—

Nothing but the burning purpose of this moment now.

Because it is for that purpose that being began.

131

free choice

Choose life!

—*Deuteronomy 30:19*

We created beings can only know that which is. That which is not, we can only imagine—or exert effort to make it happen.

But imagine a great mind from which thoughts emerge and then crystallize as the events of the physical world— spontaneously, without effort.

All events and all things—all except those matters for which this world was originally brought into being. Those are hidden thoughts—they neither emerge nor crystallize; they only unfold through our choice to do good.

When we choose life, we redeem G-d's subconscious— His most hidden desire.

132

essential good

At the core of all our beliefs lies the
conviction that the underlying reality
is wholly good; that evil lies only at the
surface, a thin film of distortion soon to be
washed away by the waves.

133

the airplane does not yet exist

A large group of visitors were preparing for their flight back to Israel when news came that the Rebbe wished to address them before they would leave. With bags half-packed, they came running to listen, wondering how they would make the flight. The Rebbe spoke at length, seemingly oblivious to the time. And then:

I know it's hard not to glance at the clock. In an hour and a quarter, your plane is leaving. Bags need to be packed, you need to bid farewell to friends and family, you need to be there on time.

But in your reality, the airplane does not yet exist. The tickets do not yet exist. Kennedy Airport does not yet exist. When it comes time for all these things to be dealt with, the Creator will cause them to materialize. All that exists for you right now is this room where we are talking.

Yes, it's hard to live this way, even though we all know it is true. But it is the only way to make the most of your time. There is only so much time in life. Whatever moment you are in, you need to be there and only there.

Because in your world, at that time, nothing else exists.

laughter, bliss, inner joy

G-d laughs. A blissful laugh. A laugh that resounds throughout the universe.

"There is nothing beyond bliss," states the ancient Book of Formation. Bliss is the origin of all being, the source of all life, the meaning behind all that occurs.

And what is bliss? It is being at self. At home. Where there is no need to go anywhere, where this moment is forever. Where there is nothing else.

Bliss is an inner laughter, so deep within that it is neither heard nor felt—not even by the one who laughs.

Think of pleasure. Of different kinds of pleasure.

There is a pleasure you take from outside of yourself. From music, from ideas, from teaching, from giving. They can provide a delightful pleasure, but they do not provide bliss. It is not pure and simple pleasure, because it is not you. A part of you delights—that part of you that is touched by this activity outside of you. But the rest of you remains untouched, unmoved.

Then there are things that ignite the innate pleasure within you. An absurdity, a joke, stupid fun. This pleasure is pure and simple because there isn't really anything giving you pleasure. You are "enjoying yourself"—something has tingled that essential sense of enjoyment you have in your own self. All of you delights.

Yet this delight cannot touch you to the core. Because it is not who you really are. And the proof—you know that you are happy. Which means that there is a part of you that remains the observer, standing on the outside. If it were truly you delighting, you would not be aware of it. You would lose all awareness of self.

But then there is the pleasure not from teaching, but from having your students beat you at your own game; not from giving, but from seeing the success of those to whom you gave; not from fulfilling your goals, but from success you had never dreamed of; not from living a good life, but from the surprise of knowing that you have lived, and there is yet more life that came from your life, and yet more, and in them you are found in a way you never knew that you knew.

This is pure bliss. There is nothing left of you to act as observer and say, "I am enjoying myself!" Because every cell of your being is engaged in this bliss. Because it *is* you.

It is the discovery of the you that you never realized you knew.

Where is that you discovered? In its fulfillment outside of you.

———◆———

In the story of the universe, each of these three sorts of pleasure plays a part:

The Creator delights in each of His creations, in every ant that crawls, in every wind that blows. It is a current of delight that electrifies all things, surging through the veins of the cosmos leaving each creature tingling with life and celebrating life.

Yet that is not a pure delight.

The pleasure that set all things into motion at the start, the beginning, the point from which all things originate and to which all things lead, that was a pure delight—because nothing yet existed but the Creator.

Yet not entirely pure, not entirely of the core-essence.

The ultimate blissful pleasure is that which we created beings give back in return—when a lost soul returns, a hidden spark of meaning is restored to its place, a piece of the world that seemed unsalvageable, ugly and sinister is transformed so that it shines— even if but for a moment—with its essential, primordial light.

All the more so when the entire world is entirely transformed.

It is then that all the universe is flooded equally with that blissful, divine pleasure, with a light that will never be withdrawn.

Because that pleasure derives from a place the *Zohar* calls "the beginning that is not known." Meaning: that which is beyond knowing. Because it is one with Him. It is that which He has chosen freely, and so all of Him is engaged.

Through His creation, the unknowable is uncovered, and G-d laughs in surprised delight to see Himself there.

All the universe resonates with that laugh.

134

two scripts

Two ways you could write your life:

"I am so small, and I make such stupid messes that even if the Creator of this magnificent universe had some plan for me, by now He must have given up. So I do too."

Or:

"I am so small, and I make such stupid messes; nevertheless, the Creator of this magnificent universe will not let go of His belief in me.

"And so neither will I."

135

nevertheless...

A young man came to the Rebbe to receive his blessing. The Rebbe looked at him and said, "A Jew must be happy!"

The young man replied, "Rebbe, what is there to be happy about?"

The Rebbe answered, "Be happy that you were privileged to wrap *tefillin* this morning!"

The young man mumbled a few words that made the situation quite obvious.

The Rebbe responded, "Be happy that you have a G-d who waits every minute for the moment you will return to Him and wrap *tefillin*!"

136

reason to celebrate

If you did good, celebrate that you have a G-d who is there with you in your good work.

And if you fell on your face, celebrate that you have a G-d who does not abandon you when you fall.

137

stories of life

Life does not tell stories. People do.

Life provides raw materials. Raw enough for us to look back and construct at least two versions of our own biography—its past, its present, and its future: one a prison, the other a palace.

This is the greatest kindness the Master of Life has given us: He has placed His own pen in our hands, so that we may enjoy the dignity of a life constructed by our own design.

138

explosive joy

Joy is an overflowing, an explosion. Something enters a person's life for which he could never be prepared, and his tidy, defined self erupts in unbounded song, dance, and joy.

Approach the Divine with a calculated mind and there is no window for joy. Embrace the infinite beyond mind and let joy hit you by surprise.

139

humble & happy

Why is it that those who hardly think of themselves are always happy, while those most self-concerned can never truly celebrate anything?

Because the more space you occupy, the less room you leave for joy.

There are those who fill their entire space with self-concern. Nothing they receive, no degree of recognition, can match the space already occupied by their self-concern.

But those who make themselves small welcome everything with joy. And if once in awhile life does not provide its bounty—well, if you don't deserve anything anyway, what is there to be depressed about?

In fact, if you feel small enough, then you rejoice when you're lacking too. Because small people don't create big issues out of things that go wrong.

Make yourself small, and there will always be room for happiness.

this is good

Who is rich? He who is satisfied with his lot.
—Pirkei Avot 4:1

With each event of life, you have a choice:

You can complain that you didn't get what you deserve; that you have a right to complain, because you are suffering...

...or you can have faith that the One above, who is good and provides only good, is taking care of your life in its every detail...

...because the good that you can perceive is only a limited good, while that which you cannot perceive as good is good beyond your understanding;

...because nothing that G-d provides you with can be bad; all that He does for you He does to lift you closer to Him, with love...

...because your faith that all is truly good heals the world, allowing the hidden good to become obvious good to celebrate in the here and now...

...and then you are rich.

Wealth, it turns out, is all a matter of interpretation.

141

not an angel,
not a beast

If you believe you are an angel, prepare for disappointment.

If you believe you are a beast, you may well become depressed.

Best to know you are human. Stay away from situations you can't handle, and when you fail, pick yourself up, say you're sorry, and continue onward.

That's even higher than the angels.

142

a soft stick

It used to be that the soul fought with the body, until one conquered the other by force.

Then the Baal Shem Tov came and taught a new path: The body, too, could come to appreciate those things the soul desires.

In the place of self-affliction and fasting, the Baal Shem Tov showed his students the way of meditation and joy. Every need of the body, he taught, could provide a channel to carry the soul high.

143

celebrating no matter what

Some gripe that they cannot reach out for G-d's help because they are not worthy.

Others celebrate that, as unworthy as they are, they have a G-d who answers their cries.

144

joyful emptiness

Start here: Open yourself to receive all that heaven wants to give you.

How will you receive it? By being empty.

Full of self-concern, of "what will become of me?" of "where is life taking me?"—there's no room for life to enter.

But a simple, open spirit is filled with joy from heaven.

145

dancing with feet

On Simchat Torah, we all dance together in a great circle with the Torah.

We are celebrating the Torah, and the Torah is something we study with our heads. But we dance with our feet, not with our heads.

If we would dance with our heads, each one would dance a different dance, each in a different space, some with friends but not with others, some as lonesome souls.

One head is higher, one is lower, one is here on earth, the other in the clouds or beyond, and some minds know only their own space that no one else can know.

But we dance with our feet, and all our feet are here on the same earth—none higher and none lower. So now we can all dance as one, with one heart, as a single being.

Now there is no loneliness, only joy.

146

real rich

To give is to be wealthy. You only truly own that which you are capable of giving away.

Yet more: True wealth begins when those you have helped no longer need you.

Yet more: True wealth is when those you have helped can say with dignity that all they have is through their own hard work.

True wealth means to lack nothing. Not money, not dependents, not recognition.

But there is great delight in seeing others thrive from your giving.

147

unimaginable journeys

Each journey the soul travels takes her higher.

Some journeys are painful, but with purpose. The purpose overwhelms the pain and transforms it into joy.

Some journeys are painful, but with no purpose in sight. There is no medicine to wash away the pain.

There is no medicine, other than the faith that every journey the soul travels takes her higher. Some so much higher, she cannot even imagine their meaning. Until she arrives.

148

the echo upstream

Waves of life flow from the heavens above, carrying with them all your needs.

Celebrate whatever comes to you, shout it out loud and with joy, and your voice echoes back with waves of even greater force.

The channels of life are widened and their currents grow strong.

149

infinite & intimate

As water [reflects] face to face, so is the heart of a man to his fellow.
—*Proverbs 27:19*

Does G-d then laugh? Does the Infinite Light cry over failure and rejoice in success? Does He who brings time and space into existence truly love with the passion of a frail human being or feel remorse as a creature trapped within the tunnel of time?

But G-d desired the human soul with all its struggles. And the proof: We are here.

And when G-d conceived this being, He looked down from His lofty realm beyond love and laughter, passion and remorse, and He said, "Shall she then be alone in her place and I in mine? Is this oneness?"

So He arranged a meeting place. He determined that the boundless emotions that are the fabric of the human soul would glimmer as well within the purity of the Infinite Light.

So that in love and laughter and compassion and awe and beauty, this human creature and G-d could find one another, and neither would be alone.

150

cursed and blessed

There is a place—the "fiftieth gate" they call it—so high that from there, all things are insignificant. There is no good, no evil, nothing can be added or taken away, the righteous are dust, the wicked are dust, nothing is of consequence, all is but dust.

Drunk with the joy of Purim, a Jew spirals higher and yet higher until he lands in that place. And there he proclaims that the oppressed have been saved, the wicked overthrown, and light, joy, happiness, and peace rule throughout the cosmos.

"As for this high place," he declares, "I am not impressed. It, too, was created for the purpose of our joy below!"

Its secret exposed, the fiftieth gate itself is redeemed.

realistic optimism

*I lift my eyes to the mountains, from whence
will come my help?*

—Psalms 121:1

People believe that only fools are optimists. But the
opposite is true.

Precisely because we understand how desperate
the situation really is, how helpless we are, and how
impossible the challenge, that itself tells us how great
a G-d we have—a G-d who can lift us high beyond the
natural order and transform the most ominous darkness
into brilliant good.

The greater a realist you are, the greater your joy.

152

take the high road

Two rivers can take you home. One flows with bitter tears of remorse, the other with sweet tears of joy.

For most of time, it was the pain of remorse that took you home. Only once soaked in those bitter waters could you rise to embrace your G-d with joy.

But now, we have experienced more than our fill of pain. That which we suffered in Europe has purged every stain, bleached every garment of our souls, refined us, and lifted us high.

We have cried enough bitter tears. Now is time to take the high road. Now is time to return with joy.

153

confusing body and soul

So you've come to the realization that you're not the stuff you made yourself out to be. In fact, you're a mess. Everything about you needs to be fixed.

But that's not you. That is the outer you. The inner you is a pure soul. And that soul is now celebrating.

Why? Because, this beast that clasps your soul tightly has finally realized what a dark pit it's gotten itself into. Which means that now there's a chance your soul can lead it back home.

And with every step the soul takes to lead the beast, with that step the soul is already back home.

Don't confuse the joy of the soul with the faults of the body.

154

the highest happiness

True happiness is the highest form of self-sacrifice.

There, in that state, there is no sense of self—

not even awareness that you are happy.

True happiness is somewhere beyond "knowing."

Beyond self.

All the more so when you bring joy to others.

inner
wisdom

Wisdom never shattered.

Within the original conception of this universe, within its design and its destiny, within that intense thought that exploded into the innumerable fragments that comprise our world, deep within was a seed, and within that seed lay the power of all that could ever be, the power of the infinite.

We call that seed *chochmah*, translated as wisdom. The Kabbalists call it "the power of what is."

The outer shell of that seed crumbled and fell. Its innumerable fragments became the principles and patterns of the universe—the wisdom of what is and what could be.

But the inner light of that seed remained whole and pure. It is the wisdom of what *should* be. It is the wisdom of *tikun*. It is the voice that Moses heard at Sinai.

The outer wisdom is the wisdom of how things work. And so, it cannot change anything.

The inner wisdom is the wisdom of what things are. And so, it has the power to change everything.

The inner wisdom descends without corruption, yet condensed and compressed countless times over, until it crystallizes in our world as an act to perform, or one not to perform. And through those crystals of supernal wisdom, all things are repaired.

In the inner wisdom of *tikun*, all things find harmony. Each spark is illuminated and shines so that every event and every object reveals its meaning. It is a vision that oversees all and discovers itself within all.

The Sages say the voice from Sinai never ended. And yet it never occurred again—because in every generation those who toil to delve into this inner wisdom and amplify its signal, unfold yet more and more of that original seed, so that more and yet more of the *tikun* can be made.

With each *tikun*, the world has changed, and now this wisdom must unfold again, to guide us in the *tikun* of this new world it has created.

Therefore, it is forever new, fresh and surprising. And yet it is forever ancient and unchanging. It is that which is beyond time, within time.

This is the Torah, which means "teaching," crystallized as the halachah, which can be translated as "the way."

Each word of Torah and halachah speaks in the same voice. It says, "This is the way things are. This is how they must be. Now go and change things.

"Change everything. Make it what it was meant to be."

———◆———

155

talking to himself

He talks with Himself, entertained by His own thoughts.

The thoughts imply a background, which is the world.

But the Torah, those are the thoughts themselves.

And we?

We are the self with whom He speaks.

156

the gift of a
broken world

Why did a G-d of infinite wisdom design a world so fractured as our own?

Why did a G-d of infinite kindness design creatures so prone to failure as us frail human beings?

So that He could share with us His deepest wisdom:

The wisdom to fix up a broken world.

157

deeper wisdom

Everything in the universe was made with infinite wisdom.

And yet, there is a deeper wisdom, a wisdom that demands you must appreciate the infinite wisdom of all things, and take that even further.

And that is to heal your part of the universe even while its heart continues to pound.

158

truth concentrate

This Torah we were given is not of the world; neither is it something extraneous to it. Rather, it is the hidden essence, the primal thought from which all the cosmos and each thing within it extends. It is not about the world; it is the world—the world as its Creator sees it and knows it to be.

The sages of the Talmud told us that the Torah is the blueprint G-d used to design His creation. There is not a thing that cannot be found there.

But that is not the essential Torah. At its essence, Torah is far beyond the world, beyond time, beyond any sort of being. G-d and His Torah are one, for His thoughts are not extraneous to Him, nor do they effect any change in Him, as do our thoughts. Rather, His thoughts, His wisdom, His desire—all are a simple oneness that does not change.

But He took that infinite wisdom and condensed it a thousandfold, a billionfold, and more, into finite, earthly terms that we could grasp—yet without losing a drop of its purity, of its intimate bond with Him. Then He put it into our hands to learn, to explore, and to extend.

So now, when our minds grasp a thought of Torah, thoroughly, with utter clarity, we grasp that inner wisdom. And when we are completely absorbed in the process of thought, comprehension, and application, our selves and beings are grasped by that infinite wisdom, which is the essence of all things. We have grasped it, and it grasps us. In truth, we become that essence.

159

the self-conscious G-d

When He made the world, He decided He would take the role of Kindness. That way, when we would be kind, we could bond with Him through our kindness.

He decided to have Wisdom. That way, by being wise, we could bond with Him through our wisdom.

He decided to be conscious of Himself, so that we could attain consciousness of that which is beyond knowing.

And all this He gave to us in His Torah. He gave us Himself.

160

the process

Torah is not simply a path by which you gradually arrive at truth.

When you are immersed in Torah, even while pondering the question, even while struggling to make sense of it all, you are at truth already.

Torah is about being truth. And then, the questions will have true answers, the struggle a true resolution.

By being truth, your destiny is yet a higher truth.

161

think His thoughts

Science is the study of those things G-d thinks about, by
one of His thoughts.

Torah is the study of G-d thinking.

be quiet

There are things too awesome to grasp,
questions to which the only response is to
be quiet, to be still, to cease to ask.

The quietness, the stillness, the
abandonment of being, that itself is an
answer.

163

raw truth

Truth is simple; it has no clothes, no neat little box to contain it.

But we cannot grasp that which has no box. We cannot perceive truth without clothing.

So Truth dresses up for us, in a story, in sage advice, in a blueprint of the cosmos—in clothes woven from the fabric of truth itself.

And then, when we have finally come to a firm grasp of that teaching, Truth switches clothes. It tells us another story— entirely at odds with the first. It tells us new advice—to go in a different direction. It provides another model of how things are—in which each thing has changed its place.

The fool is confused. He exclaims, "Truth has lied!"

The wise person listens, he is patient, and through his labor he hears a third voice, one that brings harmony to these opposites he has learned.

Until he discovers that Truth is a simple, pure light no box can contain. And so, it belongs in all places, at all times.

164

truth from the ground up

When the Creator came to create the human being,
Truth said, "Do not create him, for he is full of lies.
Kindness said, "Create him, for he will do acts of
kindness."
What did the Creator do? He cast Truth earthward,
and created the human being.
That is why it says, "Truth will sprout from the earth."
—Bereishit Rabbah 5:5.

Every argument in Torah can be reduced to the same crucial question:

Do we follow rigid, immutable truth, regardless? Or do we take into account the particulars of this situation? Do we look only from above down, or do we take the view from below as well?

The debate is never easy, because truth is no longer truth once compromised. Rather, we need to find a way to hold both ends of the stick at once.

That is why the debate must occur among us human beings here on earth, and from there the resolution must sprout. For only in that way will Truth come down to earth, where it truly belongs.

165

dark paths

He could have placed street lamps along the pathways
of wisdom,
but then there would be no journey.

Who would discover the secret passages, the hidden
treasures, if all of us took the king's highway?

166

interface

Torah is the interface between the Infinite and creation. On the outside, it speaks the language of humankind. On the inside it is depth without end.

Grasp either end and you have nothing. Grasp both and you have G-d Himself.

167

inner voice

There is an outer world and there is an inner world. As deep as you penetrate, as high as you reach, there is always something breathing inside.

The outer world is made of things. Breathing inside the things are words.

Words are the outside. Inside the words are stories.

The story is the outside. Inside the story is a thought.

Thoughts are the outside. Inside the thoughts is a great light.

At the origin of all light is the beginning that cannot be known.

The outside, that we can touch and come to know.
The inside—we must wait and be still, so that it may speak to us.

As it did at Sinai. As it does whenever we learn Torah with all our heart and soul.

168

dressed in G-d's clothes

G-d is not understandable.

But G-d ponders Himself.

And this mode of pondering Himself He gave to us, dressed in many stories and rituals and ways of life.

Dressed in those clothes, we unite with G-d in His pondering of Himself.

169

grab the clothing

The words and the stories of Torah are but its clothing; the guidance within them is its body.

And as with a body, within that guidance breathes a soul that gives life to whoever follows it.

And within that soul breathes a deeper, transcendental soul, the soul of the soul; G-d Himself within His Torah.

Grasp the clothes alone and you are like the student who hears the words but not the thoughts. Grasp straight for the soul—or even the body—you will come up with nothing. They are not graspable; they are the wisdom of an infinite Creator, and you are a created being.

Instead, examine those words and those stories, turn them again and again. As words from the heart are one with the heart, every word of these stories is Torah. As fine clothes and jewelry bring out the beauty of their wearer, so these words and stories will open your eyes to the G-dliness within them.

This is what Torah is meant to achieve: That we should discover G-d in simple stories. Because once we will find Him there, we will find Him in the simple stories of our own lives as well.

170

wellsprings

Only pure water can purify. The further you wish to take that water, the deeper your wellspring must be.

Those who wish to reach the very outside and enlighten and purify that place must reach deep into the womb of truth.

171

not about anything

People think that Torah is about something; that it comes to explain our world, what has happened and what will happen, where each thing belongs and what to do with it.

In a way, this is true. But ultimately, Torah isn't about anything—everything is about Torah.

G-d emanated light, created a world, and filled it with events, people, and things, all so we would have means and metaphors to discuss His thoughts.

172

for you

Everyone agrees with all the wonderful advice and ethics written in the books of the Sages. Everyone agrees that this is the way to run your life.

Yet each of us has our escape route, to avoid bettering our lives by changing ourselves. We ask, "Were those words truly meant for me, or perhaps for someone else in another time and another place?"

If it is truth, it is meant for you, now, here.

173

diamonds and emeralds

One man carries rocks for a livelihood. Give him emeralds and all he sees is more rocks.

Another carries diamonds with devotion and care. Give him the emeralds and he exclaims, "What beauty is here!"

Only one who values his own heritage is able to appreciate the beauty that others hold.

174

illumination

In truth, there is no need to change the world, for each thing has a place, and in that place it is good. All that's needed is a little light.

In the dark, there is no way to know what belongs in your closet and what belongs in the laundry, what is ready for use and what is in need of repair. Instead, that which could be washed and used for good is rejected and despised as hateful, and that which is clean and tidy is used for evil.

Torah is light; it tells us the place of each thing. Shine it bright and heal the world.

175

begin with alef

At Sinai, He said, "Let us bond together. Let us embrace in these *mitzvot*, commune in this Torah, and in them we will be one."

But He is an infinite, unknowable G-d. If we cannot know Him, how can we bond with Him?

And so, when He came to us in His Torah at Mount Sinai, He began with an Alef. And when we begin to learn, we begin with an Alef.

In that first, infinitesimal point of not knowing is contained all wisdom.

176

what is alef?

What is an Alef?

A point above, a point below, and a line between.

Whatever we may understand of Him is but an infinitesimal point above.

The only way we can join with Him is as an infinitesimal point below.

And what empowers us to become this zero-point below that resonates with the infinite-point above?

Our awe of Him, a line that connects below to above.

177

daily refreshments

"I know this already."

But G-d does not age! For Him, there is no "already." His wisdom is new each day.

"I live within time. Every day I am older."

Each day you are new! Each morning you are born into life again. Don't you eat again each day as though you have never eaten before? Don't you thirst as though you have never before drunk water?

"For food I hunger. For water I thirst. For wisdom I feel no thirst."

Look at those who are healthy. See how they swallow Torah as though they have never eaten before. Just start and do the same as them, and soon you, too, will be healthy, and feel your thirst for wisdom.

178

torah and us

The Torah and a Jew are one.

So much so, that even a Jew who claims he has no connection with the Torah—when pushed up against a wall, even that Jew will hold the Torah as the most precious thing in life.

179

jewish nucleus

Every society has that which bonds it: A common ancestry and a system of lineage. Or a common language, or common borders, or a governing body. Usually, it is a combination of several factors that mold a mass of people into a single whole.

The Jewish people are unique in that they have only a single nucleus— and it is none of the above.

All that bonds us is Torah. Nothing else has proven capable of holding us together for more than a generation or two. Nothing else, other than the same Torah that first forged us as a nation.

180

teaching despite himself

In the privacy of his own home, he looks in the mirror and stares shamefully. He alone knows what he has done with life. And from head to toe, things are not good.

So he asks, "I should teach others? I should provide guidance?!"

And we tell him, "Yes. Because that is your place upon this planet: We live in a time when all those who know *alef* must teach *alef* and those who know what comes after *alef* must teach that too.

"G-d Above, who formed you and put you in the here and now knows who you are, how you are and what you are capable of accomplishing. If He believes in you, you must as well."

181

holistic study

Questions are good. They show you're alive and thinking. But you're not going to get the full picture of Torah by pecking like a pigeon at crumbs on the sidewalk.

The only way to comprehend what Torah is saying is with a consistent schedule of study and a good teacher.

182

faithful questions

You don't learn by having faith. You learn by questioning, by challenging, by re-examining everything you've ever believed.

And yet, all this is a matter of faith—the faith that there is a truth to be found.

It is another paradox: To truly question, you must truly have faith.

183

faithful deeds

Examine, investigate, and question. You must, because otherwise you will learn nothing.

But when it comes to getting the job done, do it with 100% confidence that it is the right thing to do.

To get something done, you need conviction and faith. A fruitful life will not sprout out of ever-shifting sands, and its home cannot be built upon a foundation of doubts.

184

the unlikely pair

His world is woven with the threads of cause and effect; she makes her choices with no need for reason.

He questions every premise; she accepts with complete certitude.

His world revolves around his own good; hers around that which has greater gravitational pull.

Yet, without one another, neither is complete, neither can find their own essence or know their own truth.

Superficially, they seem impossibly incompatible.

At their core, intellect and faith are the perfect marriage.

185

entering the palace

Intelligence can map the journey to the palace of truth. But it dare not enter there. For within the blinding light of truth, intelligence is a nothingness, a void.

Faith is prepared to throw itself into fire for the truth. But, on its own, it cannot find its way.

Hand in hand, intelligence and faith, understanding and wisdom, find their way into the most inner chambers of truth.

186

creation,
G-dliness,
G-d

What is G-d and what is G-dliness?

We are the creation, a thought He thinks about.

G-dliness is His mode of thought.

G-d is beyond all thought.

187

paradise

Rabbi Hillel of Paritch used to say that
if the hedonists would know the ecstasy
of the divine light, they would abandon
everything to chase after it.

It is not just pleasure; it is the source of all
pleasures.

It lies waiting for you to uncover in every
mitzvah, in every breath of Torah.

188

delight unlocked

"Nothing is higher than delight," says the ancient Book of Formation.

All of our desires and musings, our every thought, word, and all we do, emerge from our sense of pleasure, our obsessive persistence for the most elegant and the most delightful.

So, too, with G-d's creation: The essence of each thing—from the tiny atom to a distant galaxy, from the majesty of a mountain peak to the depths of the human heart—is the Creator's delight in this thing as it plays its tune within the entire symphony of parts.

Hidden in the Torah is the key to that delight, the secrets to unlock the purpose and place of each thing. Use something for its purpose, direct it to its seat in the orchestra, and the brilliant glow of the Creator's delight is redeemed.

delight condensed

What is divine wisdom?
Divine wisdom is the inner delight of the Infinite, condensed and crystallized until fit for human consumption.

What is a mitzvah?
A mitzvah is divine wisdom condensed and crystallized until it can be performed as a physical action.

That is why in the study of Torah there is infinite delight.
That is why in the act of a mitzvah there is unlimited joy.

190

traditions of the future

We do not keep our traditions for the sake of the past. We keep it for their power to create a future, a power that will never end.

For the Torah was not given to this world so that it should return to its pristine glory as it was created. The Torah was given for this world to transcend itself.

i & i

If you've saved one person's life, the Mishnah teaches, you've saved an entire world.

Does that make sense? A person is just a person, a very small part of a very, very big world, right?

But the Mishnah says otherwise. Each of us is the world. Not just *like* an entire world. Not just *worth* an entire world. You *are* the world.

How is that possible?

Think of yourself. As far as you are concerned, if you are gone, everything is gone. And the same applies for every other person on this planet.

What is your world made of? Take the sum total of everything that has ever influenced or affected you. That's your world. Take the sum total of everything that affects the other guy. That's the other guy's world. Take everything that affects a cow, and that is the world of the cow. Or a tree. Or even a hammer. When you pick up a hammer, it has entered your world, and you have also entered its world. The same thing with anything and everything.

It goes further than that:

Who sits at the center of your world? You do. Who sits at the center of the other guy's world? He does (or she does). And the cow, too, sits at the center of its world.

This means that you must be aware that when you walk into someone else's life, someone else sits at the center, and you are but a satellite.

And yet we are all in the same world.

That's a very different view of reality than we're used to. Certainly, if you or I would design a world, we wouldn't do it that way. We would have one center and spread things out from there.

But this world was created by a consciousness that's beyond finite and infinite. The Creator of this world has no problem creating a finite world with infinite centers—one for every existence within it.

It's not possible for a created being to see its world from the perspective of its Creator. But we can get an idea of what it is like by trying to see our world from a different dimension:

Think of the surface of a sphere—like the globe of the earth. Before people understood that the earth was a sphere, they were all looking for the center of the map, the point equidistant from all extremes.

But now that we know we are sitting on a big ball in space, ask: Which point is the center of the surface of the globe?

Well, any point you want. And every point.

Now imagine our reality—not just all three dimensions and the continuum of time, but also ideas, emotions, experiences, pain, and pleasure—everything that makes up every conscious being—stretched over another dimension of consciousness. Just like the points on the surface of the sphere, each one of us is the center of all reality.

So you are the world. Your consciousness sits at the center of this world, and everything you know of, everything that affects your consciousness in some way or other, comprises your world.

In the Creator's mind, a world is a place of purpose. If so, nothing in your world could possibly be without meaning. If you see it, hear about it, or even just know about it, it's telling you something. And you need to do something with that.

Which explains something Maimonides wrote 800 years ago. "See yourself as though the entire world is held in balance," he taught, "and any one deed you do could tip the scales for you and the entire world to the good."

That makes a lot of sense. When you're faced with an opportunity to do something that could benefit the world—or do the opposite—everything in your world is pulling or pushing in some direction. A decision of this sort means you're now in the driver's seat. It's your turn to be the active party in your universe and do something with everything else.

So that when you say, "I'm not taking the easy way out. I'm not following the flock. I'm going to do what's right!" you are carrying an entire world along with you.

As the Mishnah continues, "Therefore, every person must say,

'The whole world was created for me.'" Meaning, "for me to tip the scales. For me to make the entire world the way it was meant to be." Because you are the world.

———◆———

worlds

Of everything G-d created in His world, not one thing
was created without purpose.
                                    —Talmud Shabbat 77b.

For every being, there is a world, different from the world of every
other being. For what is a world? It is those things of which any
single being is aware.

So that whether it be a human being like yourself, a cow on a farm
or a leaf on a tree, it knows only of its Creator, itself, and whatever
is essential to its purpose. And that is its world.

And in the world of each one of us, all that exists and all that
occurs is that which is essential for us to complete our purpose—to
fix up this world.

For G-d does not create anything without purpose.

a time for i

There are times to bend like a reed in the wind.
And there are times to act as a stubborn wall against the
tide.

There are things that lie at the periphery of life. Then
every "I hold like this" and "my opinion is..." stands in
the way of harmony and peace. Every such "I" is the very
root and source of evil.

But when it comes to matters that touch the purpose
for which you were placed in this world, that's when you
have to be that immovable wall. That's when you have to
say, "On this, I'm not going to budge."

That "I" is not evil. That's an "I" fulfilling the purpose for
which you were given an "I."

193

ego preservation

The ego is not to be destroyed. It, too, is a creation of G-d—and all that He made, He made within divine purpose.

However, that the ego must know that it is a creation, and that all He made, He made with divine purpose.

194

representatives

We are representatives of the One Above. And as such, we live as two opposites at once:

We are not beings for ourselves. We are but agents of that which is beyond us.

Yet we must be free-thinking, independent beings—because to represent the One Above, we must have our own will and our own sense of being as He does.

And if you should say, "But this is an impossibility! Two opposites in a single being!"

Yes, you are correct, it is an impossible paradox without resolution.

Which is why this renders us representatives of the Impossible One Above.

195

chutzpah

The Sages said about pride, "Excommunicated is the one who has it, and excommunicated is the one who does not."

Pride makes a mortal being into an idol. But without it, how can we change the world?

However, there is a way to harness pride: Our conscious mind must know it is nothing, and the power G-d has placed in our heart may then burst forth.

196

humble, but stubborn

The bravest heroes are also the most humble.

G-d made the heart of David and his soldiers strong and brave, so they would win in battle against Israel's enemies.

He made the hearts of Rabbi Eliezer and Rabbi Akiva stubborn, so they could traverse the highway from ignorance to enlightenment in adulthood.

They were all sensitive, humble men, nothing in their own eyes.

But G-d put a stubborn courage in their hearts—and that they would not surrender.

197

fierce & humble

To achieve wonders takes a heart both humble and fearless.

Yes, two opposites. But also from two opposite directions:

The mind awakens the heart to its nothingness. And by this, the soul G-d gave you is bared in all her brazen power.

198

empty and full

To fill yourself with wisdom, you must proceed wisely.
To proceed wisely, you must empty yourself of all wise
thoughts.

To receive blessings from Above, you must do all those
things that draw blessings.
To receive anything from Above, you must be still and
quiet.

199

a glass case

There is a place within the heart that only G-d knows. It is not something of which you are aware, or can ever be aware. Yet for its sake you were formed.

All of you must become transparent, a nothingness—so that this treasure may shine through.

strong inside

The ego is not a source of strength. It is weakness in disguise.

Inside there is invincible strength. Remove the cloud of the mind's ego, and the inner power will be free to shine.

201

who is doing what?

G-d wanted a being—a somebody—not a puppet. A creature that would decide, "This is how it should be done, using such-and-such and in such a way with such a feeling—this is what my Creator wants from me."

He gave us instructions, but instructions that demand a thinking human being.

The score is handed to us, but we play it from our own souls.

202

satisfaction

You did some wonderful things. It's okay to tell yourself that. Sometimes you have to take a step back and allow yourself some *nachat** from your accomplishments.

As long as you know that now, you get to do even better.

nachat: Hebrew/Yiddish. The feeling of deep satisfaction when someone you have invested yourself in, such as a child or a student, has done well.

the kosher ego

Do good with all your ego.

Say, "I need to make this happen."

Say, "I have to see this done."

Not only is this ego permissible, it is crucial to your mission in life.

So when does ego become evil?

When it believes it is your mission in life.

my thing

You need to feel ownership of those things most important in life—the charity you give, the kind deeds you do, the Torah you learn and teach.

You can't just say, "This is G-d's business. I did my best. He has to take care of the rest." It has to hurt when it doesn't work out; you have to dance with joy when it succeeds.

That is why G-d created the ego—so that we would do these things not as automatons, but as His agents and associates. So that we would make it our own business.

not about you

If you want to change anything in this world, you need to know it's all in your hands.

If the change you want to make is going to be real, you need to know it's not about you.

It's about what has to be done.

206

the thick lagoon of ego

He has an opinion of how each person should be, how each thing should be done. Those who follow his choreography are his friends, those who dare dance their own dance are his enemies—and few, if any, are left uncategorized.

In truth, he has neither enemies nor friends. He has only himself. For that is all that exists in his world.

"If you don't want to be so lonely," we tell him, "make room for that which is not you."

207

egocentric

He does not appear greedy, nor haughty, but an egotist nonetheless. If there are opinions in the world other than his, then people are disregarding him. If something occurs not to his liking, it is a conspiracy against him. Whatever G-d does in His world is either his reward or his punishment. All things are given meaning only as they relate to his self. He does not know of a world without himself.

So we tell him: The first step in moving forward is to leave yourself behind.

be something

The point is not to be a nothing.

G-d created you to be a something.

But not a something because you are a
something.

A something because your purpose is
everything.

be not that

If you are kind, learn also to be fierce.
If you are wise, learn also to be simple.
If you are fire, learn also to stay cool.

Whatever you find yourself being, be the
opposite as well.

real motives

No person can know his own inner motives.

He may be kind because kindness brings him pleasure.

He may be wise because wisdom is music to his soul.

He may become a martyr burned in fire because his heart burns with defiance.

How can you know that your motives are sincere? What is the test?

The test will be when doing the right thing cuts against the grain.

211

awe exchange

Embolden your awe of heaven and you will
diminish your fear of human beings.

full moon

What can we learn from the cycle of the moon, how she ever waxes and wanes and waxes again?

That a time of smallness is the means to become great,
and a time of greatness is a time to become small.

That in smallness lies the power to receive,
and in receiving lies the power to become great.

213

make up your own life

If everything were spelled out—exactly what you are supposed to do, when, how, with whom and for how long—what room would be left for you to live your own life?

This is why the details of your mission in this world are withheld from you:
Out of G-d's great benevolence, so that this little creature can decide on its own and partner with G-d in its own life.

making room

He is a very big G-d. He is everywhere.
Take up any space at all, and there is no
room left for Him.

But take no space at all, and He gives you
the universe.

215

nameless

High upon her precipice, the soul is nameless, for she has no form—she will be whatever she must be.

Peering below, beneath the clouds, she perceives a faint shimmering of her light in the deep, moist earth. There she finds form, and she calls it a name. And she answers when that name is called, for she says, "This is me."

But it is not her. It is only a faint glimmering of her light within the frame of a distant world.

216

the glimmer yearns

Below, this glimmer of a soul craves to return to her primal essence above. She yearns with an obsession beyond reason— for she knows full well that there she will once again be nameless.

Yet as metal filings are drawn to a mighty magnet, as a flame climbs upward, yearning for its own extinction, so she yearns to return.

Trapped within the fetters of time and space, held captive within body and persona, her yearning swells to its bursting point, her thirst intensifies, it cannot be quenched. Its power is fierce; it sparks and flames.

Such is the divine plan. Now you must harness that power.

With it, you can transform an entire world.

217

yearning sparks

The Holy Ari, Rabbi Yitzchak Luria, taught that each of G-d's creations, no matter how lowly, is sustained by a heavenly spark. That spark yearns to reconnect to its source—which can only happen when a human being will use it for a heavenly purpose.

If so, why does the world fight back against our every effort to rescue it, to reveal its true meaning?

It doesn't. Nothing stands in our way. A created being cannot oppose its own destiny.

The resistance is an illusion of our limited perception. As hard as we might try, we will not be able to understand why the world is behaving the way it does. The sparks themselves do not know. Because the purpose of each thing is a mystery that has yet to enter reality.

So that it is not the sparks that resist, neither is it the world enlivened by those sparks.

It is only our own sense of self, the only free agent, which says, "I will do this mitzvah. I will redeem the Divine."

"How can you redeem us," the sparks respond, "if you, too, are imprisoned within the 'I'?"

Put yourself aside. Do what needs to be done. Then, eventually, you will see that your greatest challenges, all along, were truly your greatest allies.

help
from
within

The archetype of all investments was when G-d invested your soul into this world.

Your soul began all bundled up in blissful union with the infinite light, nurtured with eternal love. And then you heard a voice:

"Come my little soul. It is time for you to leave. To descend below."

"Where is below?" you asked.

"It is a place of darkness, where only a trickle of a reflection of a glimmer of this light can enter, concealed by many veils. It is a body, a slab of meat with two eyes and two legs. It is a place where each thing believes it is a god, where ugliness beckons you, dressed in the clothing of a temptress."

"And why am I going there?"

"Because it awaits you to purify it, to fix it, to raise it to the place it belongs."

"I suppose I'll give it a try," you replied.

"You don't understand," said the voice. "You are going into that body, and your destiny is tied up with its destiny. When that body will accept your light, you will rise to a place far beyond anything you can know here above. But as long as that body remains dark, you will be trapped in the darkness along with it. Where it goes, you go."

Everything that works follows this model. Everything important in life is an investment that requires taking real risks. Everything that really matters requires putting all of yourself—investing your very soul—into the moment and tying yourself to the outcome.

Why? Because that is how every life begins, and that is what every life is about. That is how it is in business, and so, too, in every investment in life.

You cannot help another person until you have felt that person's pain. You cannot teach a student until you can hear your words from within your student's mind. You cannot bring about real change in a community unless you identify yourself as one of its members. You cannot solve any problem in the world in a real, lasting way, unless it means everything to you.

Monique Sternin, an outstanding social worker, tells of the time she arrived in New Zealand on a project to assist Maori women. One of the elder women told her:

If you are here to help me, I don't need your help, and your help is useless. But if your destiny is tied to my destiny, then we can work together.

You can only fix things from the inside out. And so, real life means living dangerously.

———◆———

Is it fair? Is it worth the risk to send a pure and innocent soul below and tie her destiny to that of this harsh world?

In truth, there is a precedent even to this archetype of the soul, and that is the very creation of all being.

An unbounded Creator could have created the world in any manner that He would so decide. But He chose that in this act of creation He would invest His very essence and being. In each thing, He would be found—all of Him.

He would suffer in the pain of His creatures as He would rejoice in their gladness. He would be lost in their confusion as He would be found in their beauty. He would be imprisoned in the cold, hard cells of their hearts as He would be redeemed in the warm pulse of their love and joy. He would lock Himself into His own creation, and He would not come out of His cell until His creatures would redeem Him from there.

That is why there is hope for the soul. And that is why it is not only fair, it is well worth the pain. Because, no matter where she goes, the soul has never left her Beloved. They are in this together.

How do you stay above it all, while investing your entire being within it all?

In the archetype, the Creator does precisely that. He does not change, even as time and space emerge from His being. He remains beyond—unlimited and perfectly free, even as He is found within His creation. Because, in His reality, none of this is of substance—it is all a nothingness; there remains only the One.

So, too, the soul, as a kind of fractal of the Creator, remains pure and divine even as she merges to become one with a human body and its animal drives.

But as we enter the world as citizens of the world to change the world, how can we stay beyond the world? If it is a nothingness to us, then what is there to change? Yet if it becomes our reality, from where do we have the power to make any lasting change at all?

For this, we are sent *tzaddikim*. Souls who stay connected directly to their source no matter where they are found. Therefore, they can connect others to their own source, no matter where they may have fallen.

A *tzaddik* is not here to do your job. The true *tzaddik*, like the soul, like G-d Himself, invests in you. And with that investment, you are empowered.

Rabbi Moshe Yitzchak Hecht was the investment of the Lubavitcher Rebbe and his predecessor, Rabbi Yosef Yitzchak Schneerson, in New Haven, Connecticut, since 1946. The demands on him grew year by year, with a synagogue, a school, a yeshivah, and many other responsibilities that required a staff several times that which he could afford.

In 1974, he wrote to the Rebbe complaining that after so many years of work he felt he was back at the same place as when he started. He simply could not continue.

He signed off the letter with a heart-rending plea: "The Rebbe should send help and do all he can."

The Rebbe responded, much as any good investor would have responded:

> *Even before you asked, I already followed your advice. I sent Rabbi Moshe Yitzchak Hecht there. But it appears from your current letter, and from the previous one, that you still are not familiar with him and with the capabilities with which this person is endowed.*
>
> *Whatever the case, you should get to know him now.*

Immediately, everything will change—your mood, your
trust in G-d, everyday happiness, etc., etc.

The *tzaddik* shows you something about yourself that you could not discover on your own. He shows you the power of your own soul. Because he sees how she is connected above.

In his last years, the Rebbe spoke about how every one of us must be that *tzaddik*—each in our own small way. We must each be one who stands above, even while entering within, shedding light wherever light will enter, connecting all those who we can reach with their own true selves.

But to do that, you need to be connected to a true *tzaddik*, one whose place is entirely above.

The Rebbe would tell the story of Rabbi Meir of Premishlan. Each day, he would climb a steep mountain to purify himself by immersing in a spring of water. Even in the snow and ice, he would climb, steadily and with ease.

The townspeople saw this feat as miraculous. But a few young men were unimpressed. One winter day, they followed Rabbi Meir, just to show that they could climb with the same ease as the old man.

And, of course, they slipped and fell.

The young men asked, "Rabbi Meir, how do you do it? Why don't you fall?"

"When you are connected above," answered the elderly *tzaddik*, "you don't fall down."

The last sparks remain to be rescued. We must travel deep within their cavern. To do so, we must stay yet more connected above. Yet higher. Holding yet tighter.

the tzaddik

The *tzaddik* is at one with G-d.

We recognize him because within each of us is also a *tzaddik* who is at one with G-d.

Inside each of us is a spark of Moses.

219

a luminous being

Some believe that life is simply about each person doing what he or she must do. For them, there are no great differences between us. One may be wise, another thoughtless, one a pragmatist, the other a dreamer, one looks heavenward, the other earthward. But, they say, life is not about thoughts or dreams or heaven. Life is about what you do.

They are right, and they are also wrong. Life is about doing, but the doing must shine. It must shine such a brilliant light that this whole world of doing will transcend itself.

To shine with that light, we must be plugged in. We must be connected together as a single organism, bonded by those souls that entirely transcend this world, as a mind transcends the body while rendering it a single whole.

Apart, we work in darkness. Together, even the simplest deed shines.

In truth, we are more than equal. We are a single, luminous being.

220

jewelry that shines

Every good deed is a precious jewel. But even the most brilliant diamond can be caked with mud. Rather than shine, it darkens—even obscures—the beauty of the one it is meant to adorn.

When you do something good, forget about the status it may bring you, forget about how good it makes you feel, forget about how amazing you are for overcoming every challenge to get this done.

Forget about any other motive in the world other than fulfilling the purpose for which you were put here by your Creator.

Do your mitzvah with love, awe and beauty. Let your jewelry shine.

221

plugged in

Good deeds, like light bulbs, need electricity.

Good deeds, like limbs of a living body, need life.

Good deeds, like a human being, require a mind and a heart.

A good deed has to connect you to your source above. If it is connected, it glows with life.

acts of light

G-d desires to have a presence in this world, and in each mitzvah we do, however it is done, He is there. But He is there in darkness.

G-d desires that His light shine in this world, and in every word of divine wisdom and every heartfelt prayer, His light shines. But it is only light, not the essence.

G-d desires yet more—that He be found here in all His essence, that which can neither be spoken nor kept silent, neither of heaven nor of earth, neither of being nor of not-being—that which transcends all of these and from which all extends.

And that is how He is found in a simple, physical deed that shines brightly with divine light.

spiritual junkies and hedonists

Some travel the path of inner serenity and wisdom, shunning engagement with this world

Others engage the world in full force, fighting day and night for their cause. To them, serenity is purposeless.

Both are following precarious roads.

The seeker is prone to spirituality addiction, abandoning his responsibility to others and to the world.

The activist is prey to the allure of achievement and acknowledgment, materialism and its pleasures, until his original goals may be corrupted and fall away.

The safe and sturdy path is to travel both roads at once. Bring wisdom into action. Act with serenity.

Yes, they are two opposite roads. But that is precisely where G-d is found.

even higher

The entire cosmos, the ancients explained, climbs ever upward.

The elements move upward, as flora transforms their energy into living, growing beings.

Flora rises upward, consumed by creatures that swim, run, fly, love, and fear.

Those mobile, loving, and fearing faunas may also be elevated, consumed into the realm of a conscious being that acts with enlightened mindfulness—a human being

And this human being, to where can it rise?

To the ultimate fulfillment of intellect and yet higher, to a place that existed before Mind was born, a place without constriction or borders.

How can any creature arrive at such a place?

Willfully consumed by the desire of his Creator, fulfilling the purpose for which he was sent to this place.

225

tuned in

There is a common misconception that the good things in life come from being in the right place at the right time. In truth, everything that is good comes from being on the right channel with the right reception.

This is what the sages call *zechut*—sometimes translated as merit. What it really means is a kind of fine tuning of the soul.

How do you fine tune the soul? You have three dials: What you are doing, what you are saying, and what you are thinking. Adjust them carefully, for static-clean reception.

226

not with toil

Not by toil, nor by struggle did the world come into being. G-d spoke and it was, a world created by words.

Not by toil, nor by struggle is the world sustained. We speak words of Torah, of prayer, of wisdom, and of kindness, and the world endures.

If so, what is the effort He demands from us?

That we invest our very essence in those words, as He invested His very essence within this world that He made.

slaying monsters together

Sometimes you might connect with someone who has a severe moral challenge in life. And you can't see how this person could possibly overcome this challenge.

But then, you have your own challenges. And you also can't see how you could possibly overcome those challenges.

Because each person has his or her own battle to fight, unique from any other.

So what should you do? You should consider the two of you to be a single person, and fight your battles accordingly.

You fight those battles that you can win—including those the other person can't handle. When you win, the other guy discovers he has won as well.

Meanwhile, the other guy will fight those battles that he can win—including those that you can't handle. Eventually, both of you will find that those impossible battles have somehow become possible.

We are, after all, a single being, all of humanity.

228

harsh or kind

When He created the world, G-d made two ways
to repair each thing: With harshness or with
compassion. With a slap or with a caress. With
darkness or with light.

"And G-d looked at the light and saw that it was
good." Darkness and harsh words may at times be
the only resort. But He never called them good.

Even if you could correct another person with harsh
words, the One Above receives no pleasure from it.
When He sees his creatures heal one another with
caring and with kindness, that is when He shines
His smile upon them.

above as below

Looking at your world from Above, all is good.

Looking at your world from within, things don't always look so nice.

Until you connect your world from within to the world above. Then the goodness flows downward without distortion.

How do you make that connection? By clinging tightly above. By putting all your trust in G-d.

230

the ingenious mudhole

There is an urge within us, at once both imbecile and ingenious.

Imbecile, because it will not look beyond its mud hole and move on.

But within that mud hole, ingenious. Because to defend its stance, it will summon circumstance and DNA, unfit parents, incompetent teachers, society, evolution, creation, low self-esteem—a myriad of excuses to avoid taking one step forward.

Every excuse but the real one: Its instinctive obstinacy that it must remain in the mud hole it knows so well.

231

pull a rope

Pull a rope, you'll see where it's connected.
Tug it, you'll see how tightly.

So, too, your trust in G-d is the entire measure of your connection with Him.

When life pulls you down, stay calm and strong, bound to your Source Above.

232

through a darkened lens

To one who wrote that she is not a believer:

You look at yourself and you say, "I am not a believer. I have no faith, no soul."

But that is not you. That is you as viewed through a darkened lens of pessimism.

To see yourself clearly, you must begin with faith in yourself. Then you will behold a spark of G-d shining within.

traveling to yourself

And G-d said to Abram, "Go to yourself, from your land,
from your birthplace and from your father's house, to the
land that I will show you."

—Genesis 12:1

If you were not you, if you saw yourself through the eyes of another,
how would you view your journeys through life?

You would see how each journey leads this person away from home.
Away from his birthplace, from those who nurtured him and that
which made him what he is. Outwards, away from himself, in so many
directions.

But you see your journey from within. From within, every journey leads
in one direction: Towards within. Towards yourself. Closer and yet
closer.

To the land in which G-d shows you yourself.

234

not listening

As a person treats others here below, so he is treated above.

Perhaps someone once tried to tell you about the ugly deeds of another. Perhaps you responded, "I'm not interested."

And you didn't listen.

Perhaps, when your soul returns to her place above, a prosecuting angel will appear to report on your deeds down here. And it's possible that some of those deeds may also not have been so pretty.

Then G-d, too, will say, "I'm not interested. I don't even want to listen."

235

the mentor

Just as some people refuse to see their faults, so there are those who insist on digging too deep, persecuting themselves over every fault and making unreasonable demands upon their lives.

Eventually they collapse from exhaustion, or worse, kick back with resentment.

This is why no person should go it alone. Everyone needs a mentor, someone who can look objectively and say, "This is where you are right now. This is what you can expect from yourself right now."

236

finding an angel

A mentor, our Sages tell us, must be like an angel.

That's a problem. Having never seen an angel, you will always be in doubt: Perhaps the mentor you have chosen is not like an angel. How can you ever rely on your mentor while so unsure of his or her qualifications?

So we will clarify: The mentor must be a human angel.

An angel, because just as an angel has no body, no hatred, no jealousy, and is not in competition with you, so the mentor must remain objective and uninfluenced by any personal benefit from the advice.

And yet a human being: With compassion, with a conscience, and with a passion for kind deeds.

237

personal trainer

All of us come with a built-in spiritual fitness trainer.

The trainer's job is to gauge our spiritual capacity at every step and adjust our program accordingly. Just when things start getting too easy, our trainer will turn up the friction on the standing bicycle or add more weights to the pulley-lift.

This innate personal trainer has many titles. It's crucial to know at least some of those titles. If you don't know the identity of this trainer, you might get the idea that you are failing when really you're making great progress.

Most popular title: "The beast within."

238

no bad roads

Sometimes you make a decision. Or you fail to make the right decision. And it takes you on the wrong road.

The choice was bad. It will take hard work to fix.

But once all is repaired and healed, there are no bad roads in G-d's universe.

Even the wrong road eventually takes you closer to the truth.

Even closer.

fix
the
beast

Not one of us is whole. We are all shattered fragments of the oneness that preceded us. If a single one of us were whole, the entire world would be whole. And if the entire world is not whole, no single individual can be whole.

But then, if we were to start off whole and complete, we would never discover who we are.

Dave had finished his masters degree in psychology and was now immersed in a course to create electronic games. He was a deep spring, bubbling with originality. I was his game design instructor.

"Dave," I asked him, "why are you switching careers in midstream?"

"Because I love gaming," he answered. "But I'm also frustrated by all the games I've played. After you've played them a little, the characters become so predictable. They're just not real enough. So I want to apply what I've learned in psychology to create unpredictable characters. *Real* characters."

"What would an unpredictable, *real* character do?"

"Probably the same as I would do. He would hack into the code and start messing with it."

"Dave, why would you want your characters to hack your game?"

"C'mon! That would be wild! I could so much identify with them. That would be the ultimate game!"

"And just how," I asked Dave, "would you render your characters unpredictable? Whatever random functions you write, at the end of the day, you have control."

And that's a problem, a grand problem for anyone who writes code to create worlds. Because there is a solution, one that extends throughout our universe. But not one that any human creator can carry through.

The solution is an explosion. Not a programmed explosion, not the product of any hyper-complex algorithm to simulate randomness, nothing any code could create. No—an explosion involving infinite numbers of infinite processes, so that the resulting equilibrium—or lack of it—could never be retraced to its source. In the language of physics, an irreversible process.

In the language of Kabbalah, that was the shattering of the world of Tohu, a world that preceded the creation of our own world. And that explosion, in turn, was triggered by the utter removal of all light at the outset of creation.

It is that curtain of darkness and the resultant explosion that allows us to act as beings of our own, to choose our destinies, to create our own lives, to take the universe in our hands. To be real.

For a human being, the problem with an explosion is that you have lost control. Anything could happen. You have let go, you have opened the box, and you will never be the owner again. All the king's men could never put those pieces back together again.

Unless you are everywhere. Everywhere, meaning that you are found in chaos as you are found in order; you are found in random chance as you are found in the predictable; you are found in every effect as you are found in the prime cause; you are found in the other as you are found in your own self.

Which is what we mean when we say "G-d."

Dave's dream was an exciting dream for any programmer. For me, it was a flash of insight.

The story of Adam and Eve with that tree in the garden now made so much sense. Why would G-d put a tree in the middle of the garden only to tell His creatures not to eat from it—knowing full well the nature He had given them—that deep human urge to taste the forbidden fruit, to break out of any box placed around them?

Now I had a grasp of the delight the Creator of the universe must have in our very humanness, our proclivity to failure, how we can deliberately fall outside the divine plan, and then somehow rewrite our script and make our way back on track—now with an even more exciting, wild, and wonderful storyline.

So here is this broken human beast.

A thousand voices scream within. Its mind and heart refuse to make peace, leaving its appetite for self-gratification to step in and take command. Battles rage daily, battles of passion, of obsession, of depression and self-destruction. Any movement forward is recompensed with mighty waves carrying it backwards and downwards with a vengeance.

And only with the greatest, most stubborn effort does it manage to escape its own nature, perhaps for only a moment, to sneak in a lone act that is pure and innocent—before it can realize what it has done.

In this one beast is the entire, broken, shattered, and fragmented world, wrapped up in a single conscious being.

And within this beast, G-d breathes. The breath reconnects the beast back to its origin, to its place that precedes the primal disaster. Slowly, step by step, the beast is revealed for its true essence and being—the intense light of Tohu.

Yet innocence lost is never regained. No memory can be erased, no failure can be undone. You can never return to the same place; you can only rise higher. Incomparably higher.

In effect, another explosion must occur. A kind of nuclear fission, unleashing the power held tightly within all matter. Once that G-d-point within the beast is touched and transformed, a chain reaction runs throughout the cosmos. Nothing remains the same.

As the *Zohar* says, "When the Side of Otherness is subdued in this world, there shines a light from beyond all worlds within all worlds."

None of us is whole. None of us must make ourselves whole. But it takes only one of us to turn our beast around, if just for a moment, and do one pure, innocent deed.

With that, all the world is changed.

G-d Himself laughs, and says, "Look what they did with my broken world!"

soul-body bonding

The human mind despises the body that houses it,
but the soul has only love.

The mind would soar to the heavens,
but for a body that chains it to the earth.
The mind would be consumed in divine oneness,
but for the body's delusion of otherness,
as though it had made itself.

But the soul sees only G-d.

In that very delusion of otherness,
in that madness of the human ego,
even there, the soul sees only G-d.

For she says, "This, too, is truth.
This is a reflection of the essence of all things,
of that which truly has neither beginning nor cause."

Therefore, she embraces the bonds of the body,
works with the body and transforms the body.
Until the body, too, sees only G-d.

240

why the heavens?

Why were we made so small, with such great
heavens above our heads?

Because He desired creatures that would know
wonder.

241

impossible

He could have made a world that was self-explanatory. It would look at itself and explain itself according to its own design.

But He made a world with such parameters that according to its own rules it cannot exist.

He wanted a world held together by wonder.

242

why is there wonder?

This wonder—this awe that you experience in a time of quiet contemplation—is not unique to the human being alone.

Every creature of the universe experiences wonder, a sense that there is something greater, out of grasp, from which it derives life.

And with that sense of wonder each thing receives life. Without it, there is no life. For that wonder is the very foundation of existence.

Why was the universe created this way?

Because without wonder, the Creator would be forever an alien to His creation.

But when there is wonder, once our work is done, the creation itself will say, "I recognize this. This is the sense of wonder within me."

243

the autograph

When He had finished His world, complete and whole, each thing in its place, the earth below and the heavens beyond,

...it was then that the Artist signed His holy name, a stillness within the busy painting, a vacuum in time, a pocket of silence within the polyphony, so that the Infinite Light could kiss the finite world, enter within and grant it life.

He called that Shabbat.

In each thing there is a Shabbat, a sense of wonder, of knowing that there is something greater, something it will never truly know, and a yearning to receive from there.

With that yearning, it receives life. Without it, nothing can survive. For that emptiness provides entry to the Infinite.

244

natural response

There is an easy path to fulfill the Torah. Not by forcing yourself, not by convincing yourself, but by achieving awareness:

A constant awareness that all you see and hear—the wind that strokes your face, the pulse of the heart beating in your chest and pumping through your veins, the stars shining in the heavens and the hard earth beneath your feet—all things of this cosmos and beyond, all are but the outer garments of a great Inner Consciousness, a projection of His will and thoughts. Nothing more than His words to us, words within which He Himself is found, but concealed.

The Master of that consciousness speaks to you and asks you to join Him in mystic union in your actions, your words, and your thoughts.

In such a state of mind, could you possibly choose otherwise?

245

practice makes perfect

Anyone can come to see a higher world. But it's not a flash of revelation from above that will take you there.

Train yourself, consistently, every day, until you become used to seeing each thing the way it is seen from above.

Real change only comes from consistent, daily practice.

246

vertical orientations

Any true wisdom, as ethereal as it may be, sits above your head as a massive reservoir of living waters. Provide it only a small opening, and it will burst into your reality and pour down into your life.

Whatever wisdom you learn, whatever you know, do something with it. Make it real.

That is the purpose of meditation and prayer—to be that bridge from wisdom to action.

247

the bigger
they are...

Nothing is true that just stays up there.
Every word of wisdom reaches its
fulfillment only when it gets down to our
real world. Lofty truths need to be pushed
over the edge to crash upon the hearts of
stone below.

Whatever wisdom you learn, open a space
in your life for that lesson to flow into and
fill.

248

meditation to part the waters

Take the world at face value, and it won't let you move forward. You'll have to bridle every impulse, carefully balance every step—and even then, for every step forward, you could fall back two. You'll have enslaved yourself within an Egypt of your own making.

Here is your route of escape—the splitting of the sea:

Meditate deeply upon the inner soul of the world;
struggle to see the vision described by our teachers.
Part the murky waters of a coarse, material world;
enter the reality that lies beneath it.

Grasp that inner vision and it will flow outward
through the heart to the conscious self,
down to the heel that steps upon the earth,
until all these, as well, become mind.

Your eyes are now open, your heart is awake,
your hands themselves know what to grab and what to avoid,
as your feet know where to walk.

In the struggle for deeper vision, life becomes effortless.

You are free.

249

the river from eden

A river went out from Eden to water the garden.
—*Genesis 2:10*

There is Eden, and there is the garden.

Eden is a place of delight, far beyond the garden, beyond all created things. Yet its river nurtures all that grows in that garden.

The garden is understanding, grasping, knowing—where all of creation begins.

Adam is placed in the garden, to work with his mind, and to discover the transcendent Eden flowing within.

So, too, that is the objective of all man's toil in this world: To reach beyond his own mind. Not to a place where the mind is ignored, but rather, to its essence, to the inner sense of beauty and wonder that guides it. To Eden.

250

G-d within

Before the Baal Shem Tov, people thought of G-d as the One who directs all things from above and beyond. The Baal Shem Tov taught that the vital force of each thing, the place from which comes its personality, its sense of pain and pleasure, its growth and life—that itself is G-d.

Not that this is all of G-d. It is less than a glimmer of G-d. Because G-d is entirely beyond all such descriptions.

Rather, that life force is G-d as He is found within each creature He has made.

251

beauty & beauty

There are two kinds of beauty, one called Tiferet, the other called Hod:

Tiferet refers to beauty that we understand.

Hod refers to beauty that inspires awe, because understanding escapes us.

This itself is something of amazing beauty: That an idea can reach down and touch a mind that cannot understand it.

How is this possible? Because at the essence of all thought lies beauty and delight. Sometimes we grasp the beauty that we can understand. Sometimes we grasp the essence that cannot be understood.

252

beyond wisdom

Perhaps a person will say, "I cannot fathom an infinite Creator, so why should I attempt to do so? And why should I attempt to awaken my heart to love of Him? What can the love of this puny creature provide Him? So I will serve Him in complete surrender, doing that which is to be done, connecting to a will and desire far beyond my own."

Such a person is wise, and he has found a deep truth. But he is wrong.

Yes, it is absurd, but G-d desires to be grasped by your human mind. Yes, it is inconceivable, but He desires to find a home within the innermost chamber of your heart, no matter how tiny that place may be. For this He created you, so that He could dwell within your world.

Serve G-d with all your heart and all your mind, because that too is His unfathomable, unbounded desire.

253

knowing that which you know

A creature born without parents can never know what it means to cry for its father and mother.

A being with no sense of the transcendent can never know what is G-d and what is divine.

The words, the explanations, we hear them through our minds, but they speak to our souls.

For the soul already knows.

254

dark knowing light

When the divine spark within us awakens to the divine, what is the wonder?

But that is not the objective of meditation, of prayer and of acts of kindness.

It is that the beast within us should lift its eyes to the heavens, that the dark side of a human creature should let in a little light, that a human ego should do good despite itself—and that is truly wondrous. How can darkness know light? How can earth know heaven?

Only with the power of He who is beyond both darkness and light, heaven and earth.

255

inspired animal

Who are you talking to inside yourself? Who are you trying to inspire?

The divine soul needs no enlightenment. The place from which she comes is a place of light.

You need to reach the beast within you. You need to bring that divine light into a language it understands.

256

wash your clothes and change

Who are you? Can you change who you are?

On the outside lies your thoughts, the words you speak, and the things you do. Those are the ways you dress yourself, your interface with the world.

On the inside lies a certain way of perceiving the world, and the emotions and feelings that flow out of that perception. Those are you yourself.

Real change can only come when that internal perception changes, but we are not masters over that place. We cannot command ourselves to perceive that which is beyond us, to feel differently from the way we feel, or to understand that which we cannot understand.

So here is a strategy that works: Just as we can wash our clothes and bathe our skin, so we can focus our thoughts, guide our words, and clean up our act. Ignore, for the time being, that a messy storm rages within. Once scrubbed enough to let light pass through, eventually your inner self will awaken to that light.

This is what Moses told his people on their last day together: "The hidden things are up to G-d. But the revealed things are for us and our children forever, to do what needs to be done."

257

fire from
heaven

When the soul awakens, she descends
like a fire from heaven. In a moment
of surprise, we discover something so
powerful, so beyond our persona, we
cannot believe it is a part of us.

In truth, we are a part of it.

258

truth for a moment

That very first tear that flowed onto your cheek—that one that fell before you became aware, absorbed in thoughts too deep to be spoken, out of the sting of awakening to what this life is truly about and what you have done with it, as you yearned to be not where you are now, not what you are now—

that tear was real, an unblemished offering. For a moment, nothing else existed, nothing but your G-d and your naked soul before Him. For a moment, it was all true.

Until, violently, you were jerked back into your world of confusion, once again in the clutches of your ego, remarking, "Aha! A tear!"—and it is as though that moment had never been. So you say to yourself, "It was all a lie. Truth doesn't pass. Truth is forever."

If anything is a lie, it is your ego, your imaginary world and its darkness and confusion. All of that comes and passes, never to return. From there, truth will never be born.

But for a moment, a glimmer of truth flashed from the world of truth into your world, achieved what it was meant to achieve, and returned to its source.

All else will disappear. That moment is forever.

259

faith, intellect & wisdom

Blind faith believes that which it is told, because it wants to believe.

Intellect believes that which it understands, because it wants to attain understanding.

Wisdom believes that which is true, because it is true.

Wisdom doesn't have to fit that which blind faith wishes to believe. Neither does it await the approval of intellect to say, "This can be understood."

Wisdom is a power of vision, the power to see "that which is" without attempting to fit it into any mold. Wisdom, therefore, is the only channel by which an Infinite G-d may enter.

260

intelligence, liberated

Blind faith is intellect's most deadliest foe. Intellect that would surrender to faith has forfeited its very nature.

True faith is intellect's most vital partner. To travel beyond its boundaries, intellect must find a vision that transcends itself.

That is the meaning of true faith: A perspective that surpasses the field of intellect's vision, a sense that there is something not only unknown, but unknowable; something before which all our knowledge is an infinitesimal point of nothingness.

And so, the mind that fears faith will choose a truth with which it is most comfortable, while the mind that has found a partner in faith will choose truth that is absolute.

261

grasping

Blind faith cannot grasp Truth, because it does not grasp anything at all.

Intellect cannot grasp Truth, because intellect is finite and Truth is infinite.

Only the eye of the soul, her inner wisdom, can grasp Truth and know it as she knows her own self. For she is Truth.

262

beyond faith & intellect

Intellect is inadequate because not all things can be explained. Intellect needs faith.

Faith is impotent because it remains forever obscure. Faith needs intellect.

But they are opposites, as contradictory as being and not being. Faith accepts; Intellect questions. Faith surrenders; Intellect struggles.

Miraculously, there is a power that can join them in harmony, and it is found in the wisdom of studying Torah: The capacity to see the truth as it is and the quietness to allow it entry without loss.

263

faith and reason

This is my G-d, and I will praise Him,
the G-d of my father, and I will exalt him.

—Exodus 15:2

When He is only the G-d of your father,
He remains exalted and beyond your world.
When you make Him your own G-d,
then you can truly praise Him with your heart.
—Shnei Luchot HaBrit, Maamar 1

Only a fool will toss out the inheritance of many generations. But one who does not take ownership remains a child.

So it is with a material estate, so it is with the faith of our fathers and mothers. We must make it our own faith, as well.

And how do you make that faith your own? Ironically, through the power of your own mind.

Engage your mind to live by your faith.

264

head and feet

With toil and persistence, asceticism and great sacrifice, a human being can enlighten his mind. He can reach so high as to perceive the world of the angels—or even to be granted the gift of prophecy.

But, as hard as any of us may try, as long as our brains are made of gray matter, we can never attain the enlightenment of the least of those fiery beings.

What amazes the angels, however, is this uncanny ability of a human being: To stick his head in the clouds and yet keep both feet on the ground. To traverse worlds.

265

simple thought

All of Jewish philosophy is but an attempt to fit inside the human mind that which is contained within the heart of a simple Jew.

It will never fit.

But, with the mind aware of its inadequacy, perhaps it can help awaken the heart from its slumber.

266

reciprocity

As much as the human soul yearns to rise up and merge within the light of her Creator, so much more so does the Infinite Creator yearn to be found within the human soul.

If so, what force could stand between them? What could hold back the Creator's infinite light?

Only His desire that this union occur with our consent, that we be the ones to crack open the door.

Even when the soul's yearning has faded, forsaking her Beloved, wrestling herself from His love and even openly rebelling...even then, He cries out to us and knocks on our door.

"Open for me just an infinitesimal pinhole," G-d pleads, "and I will open for you a vast, infinite portal to all My love, from My very core of being."

267

half & whole

To become one with another person, you must first recognize that you are but a broken half. Only then can you give all of yourself and become whole.

To become one with the Infinite Light, you must know you are but a broken half, the Infinite Light is your other half, and only then can you give all of yourself and become whole.

268

bad packaging

Every prayer of the heart is answered.

It's the packaging that doesn't always meet our taste.

269

answers in boxes

How could it be that a prayer goes unanswered?

Some will tell you that every prayer is answered, but sometimes the answer is "no."

Those who say this do not understand the secret of prayer. For prayer is when a human being below burns down the walls of his or her own ego, bringing delight to the One Above. And when delight is brought above, it must return below.

So some will tell you that, yes, the prayer is always answered, but perhaps only in a spiritual realm. Not always can a prayer affect the coarseness of our material world.

However, this cannot be, for the human being below did not pray for a spiritual blessing, but for a material one. To the place from which the prayer came, to there the blessing must return.

Rather, it must be that every prayer is answered, in our world, now, for the one who prayed and for that which he prayed.

The problem is only in the packaging—that it is wrapped up in the messy business of our coarse and dark world, so that at times we cannot see through the wrappings to discover the answer to our prayer.

But there will be a time when all of us will return to the One Above with all our hearts, and then all the concealment of this world will be shattered. The wrappings will fall away and we will see how each prayer was answered in its time. And we will hold all the blessings of all those millennia in our hands.

270

unwrapping

We pray and He answers with blessings. But we ask, "If you are already giving us blessings, why in such clumsy packages with so many strings attached?"

And He answers, "If you are giving me your innermost heart in prayer, why in such thick layers of ego? Why with such cold words? Why do you hold back your tears?"

"I'll make you a deal," He says. "You bare your souls from their wrappings, and I will bare My blessings of their clouds."

271

the paradox of prayer

Without faith, there is no prayer.

But if there is faith, for what is there to pray?

There could only be one answer:

The Infinite can contain opposites.

To approach the Infinite, we must do the same.

let him in

So strange.

We trust that He is good, and that all He does is good.

Yet we pray that He should change things.

Because to us things don't look so good. After all, His goodness is so distant from us. Beyond our understanding. Far beyond.

If so, shouldn't we simply continue to trust? To surrender to a higher understanding?

Yet He asks us to pray. To complain and to kvetch. And He listens. And He answers our prayers.

Because this is what He most desires from us: That we make room for Him in our lives, in all that matters to us as flesh and blood human beings.

And that begins when we share with Him those things that touch us most deeply. Deep within our hearts.

"Serve G-d, your G-d, with all your heart," the Torah says. The Sages ask, "What kind of service do you do with your heart?"

And they answer, "Prayer."

Pour out your heart to Him. It is the one place He can enter only once you let Him in.

in his presence

What is it that brought thinking men and women to abandon the Master for the servant?

To serve a single star rather than He who sprinkles out galaxies as dust?

To play with spiritual forces and energies rather than connect to the Source of Life?

To, even today, follow the commands of our own ephemeral cravings above the wishes of He who alone is real and true?

It is because in the worship of these we can delude ourselves that we too are something great,

and all these are made for our glory.

At the very least, we are something that must be reckoned with. We exist. Whereas in the presence of the Infinite Light, there is no room for any other being to exist.

This is the inheritance we have from Abraham, our father: The readiness to sacrifice our claim to existence so we may stand in the presence of the Infinite.

With that sacrifice, we transcend the very act of being.

274

real idols

Abraham worshipped idols, as did his father, Terach.

Abraham was an intelligent man, as was Terach.

But Abraham came to recognize the falseness of the idols, while Terach stayed behind.

Because Terach never truly believed in the idols and never truly worshipped them.

But when Abraham worshipped idols, it was with all his heart, mind and soul, every hour of the day and night.

It mattered to him. It had to be real.

Everything Abraham did mattered to him. And, therefore, he found truth..

275

true lies

In prayer, we are taught, we must stand in perfect stillness, as though overwhelmed and absorbed in the Infinite Light.

But isn't that a lie? Aren't we pretending to be something far beyond who we really are?

No—it is the truth. That is the true state of our soul, and the body reflects the soul. Everything that stands between—our minds, our hearts, and our egos—all may be oblivious to the state of our souls, but the physical body can still reflect it.

How could that be? How could the physical body reflect that which the mind and heart cannot?

Don't be so surprised. Very often the most lofty and spiritual can find no other place to be manifest but in the most simple and physical.

does he need our praises?

One time my kids outsmarted me. I had them in the van, and we pulled into a parking lot where a ferris wheel and other rides had been set up. But I had no time to take kids on merry-go-rounds on a hot summer day. I had work to do.

And then I heard from the back seat:

"Oh, thank you, Daddy! You're the best daddy in the whole world! You brought us for a surprise! Yay, Daddy!"

Five minutes later, I was frying on the hot pavement, at the foot of a ferris wheel, waving to my kids.

It was then that I understood a teaching of the Rebbe:

Before we make any request, we praise the Master of the Universe. We praise Him for the beauty of the world He has made. We praise Him for rescuing the widow, the orphan and the oppressed. We praise Him for the simple things, the lowly things, the everyday things that go unnoticed.

In that way, we are bringing Him into our world, and our prayers have an effect in this world.

277

de-kvetching

The more good news you bring your Creator, the less need you will have to complain about the opposite.

Meditate on those things you have to be thankful for. Express your thanks out loud.

The number of things to kvetch about will rapidly diminish.

the king alone

A parable of the Baal Shem Tov, of a king, who on a day of joy proclaimed that anyone who would ask anything of him would be granted his request.

Some requested power and honor, others wealth and riches. To each the king gave according to his request.

Until there was one wise person who stated that his desire was nothing more than to speak with the king personally three times a day.

The king was very pleased with this request, seeing that this person cherished the king's conversation more than wealth and honor. Therefore, he granted this request, permitting this wise person entry to the palace to speak with the king, and he also instructed that the treasures be opened to him so that he may partake also of wealth and honor.

This is what King David meant when he sang in his Psalms, "A prayer of a pauper...when he will pour out his conversation before G-d." The conversation itself is his request.

What was the wisdom of this pauper?

It is that others chose greatness for themselves, while the pauper chose to stand as a nothingness before the greatness of the king.

By doing so, he chose the King Himself, along with all of the King's greatness.

the poor advantage

Why is it the poor simpleton who has the wisdom to choose the King alone?

Because the others sit in the royal waiting chambers and are charmed by the gold and silver, the velvet and silk that they find there. Those treasures, those become their requests.

But the poor simpleton has no appreciation for treasures. So all he desires is the king alone.

So, too, it is with us: There are treasures of the mind, treasures of the soul, treasures of the higher spheres.

But we poor simpletons desire none of these.

We desire only to join with the One who made all things, great and small.

we are the poor

We are the poor man of the Baal Shem Tov's tale.

We are poor of vision, because our eyes are blind to wonder.

We are poor of heart, because we cannot delight in the ecstasy of that wonder.

We are poor of soul, because this materialistic world has robbed us of any sensitivity to that which can neither be seen nor touched.

And because we are the poor man, we will not be satisfied with wonder, with ecstasy, or with anything spiritual or even divine. We will only be satisfied when we have the King alone.

Nothing else will placate us. Nothing, until, in every corner of our world, we find only Him.

learn as a child

Intuitively, we imagine the child as a dependent, a pupil, an adult in the making. As though the child is only becoming, not yet being. We invest in the child, not for what the child is now, but for what the child will become.

But the child is now.

If we do not learn from the child, we are not living in the now. We have cut our roots that nurture us from our past. How will we grow into our future?

If we cannot learn from the child, we are not adults. We are old people. We do not grow; we only age.

To grow is to build upon that with which you began. Leave the child within you behind and you are a nomad without a destiny, wandering in circles through shifting sands that leave no trace of your footsteps and only portend your eventual demise.

Listen to the child, learn from the child, and you are a towering tree anchored and nourished by deep roots, forever supple in the wind, sprouting new leaves, twigs, and branches whenever the sun glows.

Because as much as the child needs the adult as a nurturer and a guide, so, too, we adults need the child to return us to our innocence, to the point inside from which we first sprouted, and from where we still receive life. Which perhaps explains why the Rebbe again and again taught us to think as a five-year-old child.

The Mishnah defines wisdom as the capacity to learn from anybody and everybody. For "there is no person who does not have his time, nor any thing that does not have its place."

For the world is a constantly revolving sphere, each point the very pinnacle of that sphere in its unique way. So that there is no being that receives and does not give, just as there is no being that gives without receiving. There is no time in life that is only a preparation for a later time. And there is no person who is only here to become someone else.

A woman is a woman and a man is a man. A teacher is a teacher and a student is a student. An adult is an adult and a child is a child. And yet all of us provide, all of us teach, all of us nurture—each in a way no other can.

This is *tikun*, this is a revolution that is forever: When there are no one-way streets in our world. When each thing finds its purpose in this moment now.

When we can hear the deepest wisdom in the simplicity of the child.

281

a child each day

The wise person begins each day as a small child. Every cell of his being is dedicated to learning wisdom, and so from every person he finds some wisdom to learn.

Each day, he rises to great heights of wisdom. And yet, the next morning, he begins all over again, as a small child, in wonder.

282

learning the
child

There are no one-way streets in our world. There is
no one who gives without receiving, and there is no
one who receives without providing something back
in return.

So it is with the child. Just as the adult gives the
child the knowledge and wisdom of life, so the child
shows the adult how to live it to its fullest.

283

true naivety

What is it that the child has to teach?

The child naively believes that everything should be fair and everyone should be honest, that only good should prevail, that everybody should have what they want, and there should be no pain or sadness.

The child believes the world should be perfect and is outraged to discover it is not.

And the child is right.

284

childish
teaching

A child cannot learn something without running
outside and screaming it to others.

And so it should be with all those who have
knowledge.

285

the engaged child

Watch a child involved in any activity.

Whatever a child is doing, there is the child, the whole child.

286

childish demands

When a child feels something is missing, the child wants it, demands it with all his heart and soul—and demands it now.

We are G-d's children.

The world is not the way it should be.
None of us are in our proper place.

We need to demand that He fix all this.

We need to scream out from our hearts, as a small child would scream.

We need to plead that He fix it now.

287

childish enthusiasm

A child's enthusiasm comes in a storm, taking over the child's entire world. That is why, when a child embraces a new, good way of being, it enters forever, and nothing can ever take it away.

childish love

A child gives love for the sake of love.

But even an adult can learn to do the same.

289

childish delight

The child delights in the simple things of life.

Yes, sometimes delight can take you in the wrong direction, and yes, we have to steer the child away from that.

But delight itself is good.

To live is to delight in life, like a child.

290

preserving the child

How will we preserve the innocence, the genius, and the beauty of the child into adulthood?

First, we will nurture that beauty from its very beginning. We will surround the child with Torah and sing to it songs of wisdom even before it leaves the womb. We will help the child make his or her room into a sanctuary with holy books, a place to say prayers, and a charity box fixed into the wall, to be used daily.

And then, as the child emerges to discover that the world outside is not quite the same as that sanctuary, we will explain:

"Yes, this is not the way it is supposed to be. But it is only temporary. You and I and all of us, we are going to change it. We will make the whole, big world like your little world—a sanctuary."

291

nuclear power

When it comes to education, there are four things we can learn from the harnessing of nuclear power:

In normal times, it's enough to derive energy superficially. But in these times, on the verge of the messianic era, we need to tap into the innermost, nuclear powers of the heart, mind and soul.

Real change comes from within each person. The job of a teacher is only to provide a trigger from time to time, one that leads to a chain reaction of growth and learning.

The greatest challenge of harnessing nuclear energy: Once you start a nuclear chain reaction, you must stand by and moderate, so that the energy goes in the right direction.

Nuclear reactors must pay back many times the investment. Each one of us must contribute back many times over that which we have been given.

all teachers

In our times, it is crucial that every Jew who knows anything must be a teacher to others.

If you know *alef-bet*, teach *alef-bet*.

If you know only *alef*, find someone to whom you can teach *alef*.

But all must teach.

293

learn & teach

Learning means to teach; teaching means to learn.

Immediately upon learning, you must teach. As you teach, you must learn.

When you study, even if you have no one to teach, study as though you were preparing a class.

Then it will be real learning, and certainly you will merit to teach it.

already heard

I was in the midst of the exile, on the river of Kevar.
—*Ezekiel 1:1*

(Kevar is also the Hebrew word for "already.")

At the onset of the exile, Ezekiel sat on the bank of a river called "I heard that already."

It is a river so cold, it can make icicles from fiery sparks of wisdom.

It is a river so putrid, the most wondrous secrets become old and rotten there.

It is a river of exile. Because it is a lie.

Wisdom never says, "I heard that already."

If you had truly heard, if you had absorbed this wisdom deep within your soul until it meant everything to you, it would be new to you each time you heard it again.

295

there with the student

The Talmud states that when a student is exiled, his teacher must be exiled with him. Not simply that he must go with him. He must be exiled with him.

Which tells us: If you truly want to teach, you must put yourself in your student's space.

If your student has wandered far astray, tear yourself away from your own space; feel what it is like to be distant. If your student is in pain, let that pain become your pain. There must be nothing that lies between your student's world and your own.

Teach in this way and you can bring even the most distant student to your own level of understanding. And yet higher: You will learn from this student that which you could never have learned from your own teachers and colleagues.

296

don't wait to be asked

There are those students who come to you and ask for guidance. And there are others who sit quietly and do not ask.

Don't assume that those who are in need of guidance are the ones who ask. On the contrary, the very fact that a student does not ask tells you that this child is most in need of guidance.

A teacher must go to the student, awaken the student, and say, "Why don't you bother me, my student? Ask me. Speak to me."

297

your own tradition

Nobody believed Noah. But Abraham, some say, convinced most of his generation.

Noah spoke as someone who followed a tradition of the past. Abraham described how he had discovered G-d on his own.

You can only give it to others once you have made it your own.

a mighty arm

When a child learns that G-d struck the Egyptians with a mighty hand, no matter what his teacher may attempt to explain, he imagines a mighty hand reaching out of the sky. Because that is the world of the child.

When a child learns that Abraham argued with G-d, no matter what his teacher may explain, he imagines Abraham speaking with G-d like a man speaking with his friend. Because that is the world of the child.

When the child grows older, he will understand that G-d does not have a body in the way that any creature has a body.

Growing yet older, he will understand that G-d does not have an existence in the way that any other entity exists. He will learn that G-d is infinite and unbounded.

And yet, when he was a child, he learned the truth. Only truth.

Because in the world of a small child, a mighty hand stretched out from heaven is the power of the Infinite.

Indeed, in the simplicity of the child's imagination is a truth the adult can only envy.

299

we are the child

There is you,
there is everybody else,
and then there is your child.

The child is not one of everybody else. The child is you.

Yet the child is not you, the child is someone other than you.

The child is both—for the child is born of the essence that transcends you and other.

We are children of the Infinite Light.

growing up

There is a time when He relates to us as a father relates to his infant child. We can cry and spit up and make those little messes babies make—but He loves us, just because we are His child.

And then there comes a time when we have to grow up and actually do something all our own.

301

ungraspable

All our philosophy is meant only to achieve some sort of grasp of what a small child means when he prays to G-d.

But we can't.

As soon as we grasp, it is gone.

wonder

Rabbi Bere Wolf Kozhevnikov, rabbi of Yekatrinoslav over a century ago, told a parable:

Imagine yourself strolling through an art gallery. You find three people sitting on a bench before a large painting. One enthused, one annoyed, and the third in utter stillness, mesmerized.

So we'll call them that: Enthused, Annoyed, and Mesmerized.

You ask Enthused, "What's so exciting? It's just a painting of a bird in the forest."

Enthused answers, "Just a painting? It's magnificent! See how beautiful the artist made that bird! So realistic! So perfect in every way!"

Now you turn to Annoyed, and ask, "What's so annoying? Isn't it a beautiful painting? Look how lovely the bird and the trees are!"

Annoyed answers, "Beautiful, shmutiful. Listen to me, I know the artist personally. The artist is a person of deep spirit, a sage in all ways, a master intellect who outshines all the great thinkers of our time. And for this such a great mind should be renowned? For a colorful painting of a silly little bird upon a tree?"

Fair enough. Now you turn to Mesmerized. "Excuse me! Ummm, Mr. Mesmerized, hello! HELLO!"

Finally, Mesmerized turns and stares at you, slowly coming back to this world. You say, "Really sorry to disturb you, but, you know, you really shouldn't be so mesmerized with this painting. If you would know the artist, well, he's a great philosopher, a deep thinker, and . . ."

"Yes," Mesmerized interrupts, "I know the artist well. He is my teacher and mentor. And I am amazed how such a great mind has managed to fit all his genius into the details of such a simple scene of a bird upon a tree."

We dwell within a living work of art, perhaps a symphony, or perhaps a dance, of uncountable parts. Where do we find the Artist within His art?

Ask a scientist. He might say, "Look in the elegant mathematics of physics, in the rhythms and patterns that play throughout the universe. There is such order and harmony; we can reduce a massive universe to only half a page of calculus. An entire universe in such a perfect, unified, and elegant design!"

But ask a prophet and he will scoff at the scientist. "Is a composer judged by the skill of his counterpoint? Is a musician judged by the agility of his fingers? You count and measure, and with this you claim to know wisdom? What tight box have you scientists made for the soul of the universe, a free soul in the most ultimate sense of freedom? The unknowable source of all being cannot be measured between your calipers."

"Rather," the prophet will say, "the Author of this universe can only be known by His miracles. For in them He displays that He is not bound to any pattern or mathematical law."

Which is what people say: "If I would see an open miracle, then I would believe."

But it is not true. If they would see the sea split, the dead come to life, the sun stop in its tracks, they would blink their eyes, shake their heads, and eventually get back to the same old life.

What you cannot comprehend, you do not see. It may as well have happened in a different world. It has nothing to do with you. So that miracles alone are not a path to knowing G-d.

That is why, some 500 years ago, Rabbi Yitzchak Arama wrote that there is another way to perceive the infinite Creator. If we look with open eyes, we will discover the signature of an unknowable Creator within the patterns of nature we know so well. We will see and we will comprehend the impossible.

And we have.

For one thing, we have found universal constants. Which is a great puzzle. Our universe is composed of finite parts, constantly moving, decaying, and restructuring. How is it that in every part of the universe we observe, and for all of time that we can surmise, the gravitational constant remains the same, the ratio of light, energy, and mass remains the same, along with several many other mysterious numbers that never change in a universe defined by change?

Rabbi Arama would answer, "Aha! The signature of the Artist, an unchanging G-d."

Then there is infinite depth. Within the chaos/complexity of nature, within the incessant throbbing of life ever-oscillating throughout this huge matrix of energy fields we call a universe, peering through our telescopes and microscopes, we gasp in wonder at the endless wisdom the Grand Artist has invested into the finite details of this place—so that any splotch of dirt contains enough information to keep a laboratory of scientists busy for eternity. Infinite information in every finite detail.

There are fractals within nature—symmetries that defy measurement, containing within themselves infinite depth. All matters at one time considered pure fantasy or hypothesis, yet today observed ubiquitously, even applied in technology.

Today, we are forced to recognize that almost all the numbers in the universe are irrational numbers. Numbers that cannot be stored—yet we can see them before us.

Long ago, the Mishnah said it, and Maimonides explained it: Take a square of 50 square feet and tell me the length of its borders. You cannot—the number cannot be written. Just as pi cannot be written. Just as the square root of 2 cannot be written.

Before our eyes, we see and we understand that which can be neither said nor known.

If Rabbi Arama were alive today, he would point to a cell of a living organism and say, "See the complexity of this single cell, which scientists have only begun to fathom. A thousand factories at work with marvelous machines, all coordinated to work together with precision. See how it is even capable of healing itself—a miracle our logic tells us must be impossible. Yet more impossible—see how a system more complex than an entire metropolis can reproduce itself within only four hours!"

"Endless wisdom, infinite wisdom," he would say, "packed within tight, finite packages."

> *"It always bothers me," said the legendary physicist, Richard Feynman, "that, according to the laws as we understand them today, it takes a computing machine an infinite number of logical operations to figure out what goes on in no matter how tiny a region of space, and no matter how tiny a region of time. How can all that be going on in that tiny space? Why should it take an infinite amount of logic to figure out what one tiny piece of space/time is going to do?"*

"Yes," answers Rabbi Arama, "the paradox of the infinite within the finite."

And endless freedom. Yes, there are patterns—but patterns alone do not make beauty.

As Nobel laureate Ilya Prigogine points out, within every tidy pattern of nature we find unpredictable chaos. Within every symmetry of nature there is a Mona Lisa smile, something just slightly off, tucked into the form of every leaf of every tree, every hair of every tiger, every cloud in the sky, every stream of water upon the earth.

The symmetry breaks itself, only so slightly so as to retain its symmetry, just enough to grant it beauty—so that you can look, look again, and again, and never cease to be surprised.

—◆—

Thank you, Rabbi Arama. The Artist's signature is there. Not just a deep artist, but an infinite Artist resides within the finite, the unchanging within constant change, chaos within order. And that is true beauty—beyond whatever any open miracle could provide.

And yet we have still not touched the Artist's soul. He remains the Grand Architect of the universe that houses us. We stand in awe and wonder. But that is not enough. We want Him, the Artist Himself.

That, after all, is what the artist does—he plays not his instrument nor his part, but his audience. He spills out his guts, so that you have all of him.

For that we must look in another place. For that we must look in the small miracles of daily life.

You've been there—many more times than you can remember. Those instances where by all predictions, there was no way out. Whether it was the doctors, the lawyers, the accountants, or the mother-in-law, all prognostics pointed in one direction, and it wasn't a happy one.

And then, things unfolded, smoothly and seamlessly, so that the entirely unexpected occurred and all ended well.

No laws of nature were broken. Little, if anything, escaped its normal patterns. And yet, it was obvious that your life was managed directly by the Manager of all things, who gets whatever He wants, no matter the situation. And He gets it without having to change a thing. Because He is everywhere, in both chaos and in order.

A Jew in his prayers thanks G-d three times a day for "Your miracles and wonders with us each day." The rabbis say that every day, miracles occur to us that are greater than the splitting of the Red Sea.

But we are blind to them. We see G-d face-to-face countless times a day, and we are in denial. Cognitive dissonance blocks out the signal. We simply cannot accept the paradox, that in a natural, orderly world, its Creator is getting whatever He wants without disturbing a thing.

What is an artist? An artist is a free soul.

What is art? Art is a free soul expressing itself in finely-tuned, disciplined articulations.

That is why, in his art, the artist discovers himself—for he discovers that he is not a prisoner of his freedom. He discovers a place within himself where freedom and discipline are not in conflict—they are one.

And that is beauty—a window to something so intimate, so essential to his very self, the artist himself was incapable of knowing it. Until he created his art.

Ask any true artist, "Who are you, really?" He will point to his art. Not so much the art itself, but the act of creating that art. And that is something you can only experience from the inside. As does the artist.

And so, the Grand Artist has placed us inside His art. That is His act of love to us—to allow us to find Him within His art. To find Him as He transcends all bounds, within the tightly bound drama of our everyday lives.

Now we grope in darkness. But we are creatures of a twilight just before the dawn. Soon, a new sun will rise, the darkness will vanish, and we will awaken to see with open eyes. And we will see that the Artist, in all His essence, was always there with us, carrying us through our journey. Not with our minds alone. The muscle, fat, and bones of which our bodies are built will sense the infinite G-d.

That, after all, is what the prophet Isaiah foresaw when he said, "All flesh shall see."

The dawn is upon us. The sun will soon rise. Open your eyes, open them and see that everything is already here.

———✦———

302

greater miracles

There will come a time, very soon, when we will be shown miracles so great, they will make the splitting of the Red Sea appear as ordinary as nature itself.

So great, no mind can begin to fathom them; so powerful, they will transform the very fabric of our world, elevating it in a way that the wonders of the exodus could not achieve.

For then, our eyes will be opened and granted the power to see the greatest of miracles: Those miracles that occur to us now, beneath our very noses, every day.

showing miracles

As the days when you left Egypt,
I will show them wonders.
—Micah 7:15

There is a prophecy, not about miracles that the Creator will perform, but about those that He will show.

He will only need to show them, because they have already been performed. He performs them countless times every day, within the minute details of our lives.

They are the greatest of miracles. So great, they escape our perception. For our minds are incapable of perceiving a boundless G-d within the neatly bounded order of a physical world.

Until the physical will have been transformed through our labor. Transformed and made transparent, so that these most ultimate of wonders will shine through.

Our world will be a lens to perceive the infinite.

304

unnatural
response

The philosopher, when he sees a miracle, looks for a natural explanation.

The Jew, when he sees nature, looks for the miracle.

305

the boundless leaf

What is a leaf? A leaf is infinity compressed within a finite creation.

It is infinite because its very existence is an act of a Creator who knows no bounds, who can extrude an endless number of leaves in endless variety out of the nothingness.

It is infinite in design, containing a wisdom that may be studied for endless lifetimes and yet never depleted.

It is infinite in form, for there is nothing about it that can ever be measured and stored with perfect accuracy, nothing of its future that can be predicted with precision.

And it lies within a context that is boundless, the boundless destiny of all creation: that the Unknowable should be made known from His hiding place within a single leaf.

306

miracles

At every moment, in each thing, a miracle occurs that far transcends even that of Moses splitting the Red Sea: Existence is renewed out of the void, and a natural order is sustained where there should be chaos.

Indeed, it is not the miracle that is wondrous, but the natural order. Does anyone have a good reason why gravity should behave today the way it behaved yesterday?

307

the symphony &
the conductor

What are the laws of nature?
A symphony of innumerable parts
following rhythms and patterns in
wondrous harmony.

What is a miracle?
The Conductor baring His hands.

prophecy

G-d speaks with us at every moment. His words form all the events of time and space we see about us.

What then is a prophet?

Nothing more than one who catches those words in their ethereal form before they crystallize into the events of time and space.

pocket protection

Our minds sit nestled in a pocket of natural events,
sewn with the thread of inexplicable miracles.

The pocket protects us: Exposed to the raw light
of those miracles, we would be paralyzed with awe,
incapable of continuing with life.

310

related to wonder

Yes, there is wonder in the world, but we do not stand on the outside gaping in.

This wonder is our parent. We, the Jewish people, are its child. It is our G-d, and we are its people.

311

sustained wonder

This is the meaning of a Jew and of Judaism—the very meaning of these words:

To live in wonderment. To acknowledge that which is beyond our grasp. To know that the very existence of anything is beyond understanding.

And then to strive to understand.

312

splitting the sea

Along the path to Torah is the splitting of the sea.

The sea is a deep, murky place of materialism under which lies submerged the divine soul. With a miracle, it is ripped away and the soul can sing. Only then can the Torah be received.

Don't imagine you can preserve your belief in a materialist world and append to it a Torah consciousness. The sea of materialism must part and the world must be seen for what it truly is: A wondrous place ever-awaiting miracles.

313

real time

Something is true, we say, when it actually happened in our physical world.

But some events are even more true than that; so true that they are not limited to a certain year in a certain place. Instead, they occur again and again every year, wherever we are.

They are the days we celebrate every year, in a very real way in our physical world.

314

walking miracles

If you are seeking an open miracle in our times, you have not far to look: Any Jew alive on the face of this planet today is a walking miracle.

Our mere existence today is wondrous, plucked from the fire at the last moment again and again, with no natural explanation that will suffice.

Each of us alive today is a child of martyrs and of miracles.

315

being & not being

He made His world of contradictions, opposites that combine as one.

At their nexus, a world is formed: Neither can exist without the other, all function together as a single whole.

Being and not being,

infinity and finitude,

light and darkness,

form and matter,

quantity and quality,

giving and withholding,

the whole and the fragment,

the community and the individual,

miracle and nature.

They are mere modalities—He Himself is none of them. He mixes and matches them at whim.

Paradox is our window upon the Unknowable.

316

from beyond, with love

A miracle is what occurs when a force from beyond our tightly defined little world enters within.

That is why to see a miracle, an open heart and an open mind is not always enough.

You need to put your own mind and heart aside before that which is so far beyond you. And then you will have eyes to see.

317

change

That which can be grasped will change.

That which does not change cannot be grasped.

318

the unnatural nature of things

He could have made a world where the nature of each thing could be deduced from its parts. A predictable, orderly world. A world void of wonder.

And then we would say, "Things are this way because they must be this way." G-d would be a stranger in His own world.

Instead, at every phase, a whole new world emerges, one we could never have predicted from anything we knew before. Until we must conclude that our finite world somehow contains infinite possibilities, that both nothing and everything is possible, that things are the way they are only because He desires they be that way.

He has made our world wondrous, so that it has room for Him.

319

playing with our minds

If He had made the world a complete and utter
mystery, we would have no path to know Him.
And if all would fit together like a neat and tidy
grandfather clock, we would not know that there is
anything more to know.

So He took His raw, unknowable Will and cloaked
it in wisdom, and through that wisdom a world was
formed. And in that world, we sentient beings are
drawn to explore the wisdom—only to find ourselves
engulfed within an unfathomable ocean of wonders.

Now it is within the mind's grasp to know that no
thought can grasp Him.

320

delight and quintessence

A bird builds its nest, a tree spreads its bows, a cloud floats across the sky—and we see there beauty, ingenuity, wisdom, and might.

But behind it all is delight. The delight the Creator takes in each thing.

Each thing begins with delight; delight condenses to become wisdom; wisdom condenses to become ingenuity, consciousness, love, might and beauty, and all the other fabric of the universe.

"Nothing is higher than delight," says the Book of Formation. It is the quintessence of all that exists.

321

engaged

Our job is to keep Him engaged. When the Creator's mind is engaged, our world comes alive. It resonates with His presence. Miracles happen.

If we lose His interest, He acts as though He is not there, as though He is sleeping. Madness breaks loose.

He needs to see things that interest Him happening down here. Something more than an everyday world going about its everyday stuff. More than the patterns and rhythms of the nature He created.

Even angels singing His praises all day in fiery ecstasy—that is their nature, as He created them, simply unfolding as it should. Nothing is truly changing, nothing moves forward.

But an earthly being doing a heavenly act—now that's something to wake up to.

322

the unknowable you

You are He who is G-d alone; You made the heavens, the heavens of the heavens and all their host, the earth and all that is upon it, the seas and all that is within them, and You vivify all of them...

—Nehemiah 9:6

There are three ways by which we know the unknowable You:

Your light emanates without end, bringing forth infinite universes filled with infinite creations, each creature designed with infinite wisdom and sustained by Your infinite power. Therefore, we know You as "The Infinite."

Yet You are more than that.

You remain ever-shrouded in darkness, for if Your

322 *cont'd*

presence would be felt, not one thing would remain in existence before Your light. In truth, there is nothing else but You. And so, we know You as "The Absolute Existence."

Yet You are more than that.

Within this world of concealment, within the discrete and limited bounds You have set for it, the infinite, absolute You is with us at every moment of need, alive within the small, seamless miracles of our lives—those we rarely notice.

For You transcend knowing and not knowing, revelation and concealment, miracle and nature, finite and infinite, being and not being, light and darkness. And You are found in all of these at once.

Therefore, we know You as You,
for there is nothing else we can say.

323

nature, miracles & beyond

What is natural law? Natural law is when the Director directs each of His actors according to its character. Wondrous, but sensible. G-d has endless wisdom.

What are miracles? Miracles are when the Director does whatever He wants, disregarding the character of His actors. Amazing, but why not? G-d is free.

Then there are the greatest of miracles: When the Director does whatever He wants, contrary to the character of His actors, by directing each one according to its character.

Does that make sense to you? Can it be?

There is no room in our minds for such miracles. They are a perfect paradox—freedom and wisdom, chaos and order in perfect harmony. Therefore, we rarely can admit that they have occurred.

But go beyond your nature to fulfill your mission in life and you will ride the waves of such miracles, and the entire world will see with open eyes.

324

mystery by design

What is wondrous about nature is that it explains itself, and the more it explains itself, the more mysterious it becomes.

Each thing says, "I do this because I am this way." As though each were its own being, guided by its own design.

Until a pattern emerges, and a greater pattern, and yet greater, until a wondrous wholeness emerges in which there are no things. There is only one.

Nature reveals its oneness through the art of concealment.

325

simple purpose

This is all that life is about, why you are here, and why you were created:

To experience every detail of life as a personal affair between you and the Creator of all worlds,

to believe that every step you take is guided by His loving hand,

and to know that you lack nothing, because He is good.

healing begins at home

There's a story about a man who was lowered down a deep shaft, lower and lower, until the darkness was so dark he could touch it with his fingers, the damp so damp it seeped through his bones, and the cold so cold it made those bones shiver. And all around was nothing but mud.

Finally, without warning, he hit the hard rock bottom.

When they pulled him back up, they asked, "What did you find down there?"

"It was cold," he answered.

"What else?"

"It was dark," he answered.

"What else?"

"What else do you want?" he answered. "I hit rock bottom and it was cold, dark, and full of mud!"

"We know it's full of mud!" they retorted. "It's a mine! Now where are the diamonds?"

If you read the introduction to the chapter on *Tikun*, you may have already figured out the story. It's about us, about how our souls come down to a fractured, light-deprived world.

If you don't know why you're here, sometimes all you can see is mud. And there's no shortage of mud in this world.

But if you know you're here on a mission, the supreme mission to rescue the lost divine sparks and repair the universe, and if you know that the most brilliant, precious stones are to be found in the darkest, deepest places—then the mud becomes almost irrelevant. All you see are diamonds.

The first place to look for those diamonds is in your own home. Then in your community.

Once you can find them there, you'll see diamonds everywhere.

—————◆—————

326

harmonization

Harmony at home is a matter of emphasis:

Let dissonance slip by.

Celebrate beauty.

327

home improvement

Harsh words, demands, and ultimatums—these shake the very foundations of a marriage and a home, tearing its walls apart until each person and each thing stands alone.

Gentle words, understanding words and listening words are the trunk from which a marriage grows; the foundation upon which a home stands. This is the sweet and pleasant path of Torah.

A home cannot be repaired unless its foundation is firm. Once a couple learns to speak as friends, their marriage can endure everything, forever.

328

give & take

Marriage is not a power struggle, and the home is not a battlefield. To give in does not mean to relinquish power, and talking things over does not mean you are entering negotiations.

The two of you comprise a single entity—a couple. What is good for one is good for the other. When you make a decision, it is the decision of both of you as one being. Do it not as a sacrifice but as a gift, not as a defeat but as a triumph of love.

329

learn together

Every couple must have a set time to study Torah together.

What should they study? Something that interests both of them—such as the Torah portion of that week, or something about the approaching festivals.

330

the giving relationship

In a home, in a relationship, in any situation where people work together, each side has to give.

What you give is not so important. It's how you give. You have to want to give.

331

home

A home is more than a house; it is a state of being. A home provides space and shelter, not just for bodies, but for the human spirit.

Who creates this space? Mainly, the woman. As it says, "A feminine wisdom builds her home" (Proverbs 14:1).

332

wisdom, not hammers

"A home," wrote Solomon the Wise, "is built with wisdom."

And not with a hammer.

Because wisdom is the glue of beauty. Wisdom, meaning the ability to step back and see all of the picture, the past and—most important—the future to which all this leads. To see the truth inside each thing.

Without wisdom, there are only fragments. With wisdom, there is a whole. And there is peace between all the parts of that whole.

333

the only child

Why do parents love their children?

Because the lower world reflects a higher world. And above, there is a Parent and He loves His children.

Why do parents of an only child have such unbounded love for their child?

Because this is the truest reflection of the world above: Above, each one of us is an only child, and His love to us is unbounded.

334

meditation on a scolding

Before you scold a child, stop and think of who this is and where you stand.

This is a child of the Creator of the Universe.

And you stand before Him, scolding His child.

335

unnecessary evil

There are times when a stern word is necessary, when a child needs a firm reminder, when social justice demands harsh measures.

Of their own, these acts are unwholesome—only their context redeems them.

Think of them as toxic medicines, to be administered with great care. Once they are no longer necessary or can be replaced with more wholesome means, they are no longer medicine but poison.

336

who this
really is

What you see of a person, you may not like.

Yet who this person really is, you can never know.

Speak to that: Look past the outer shell and talk to the unknowable inside.

Talk to the soul, and she will hear.

337

unreacting

The nature of a human being is to simply react, to throw back at others the medicine they mete out to you.

Rava, the Talmudic sage, would say, "Resist the urge to return bad with bad, hurt with hurt, scorn with scorn—and the heavens will overlook your own scorning, your hurting, your acts that were not good."

G-d shadows man. Go beyond your nature with others, and so will He do with you.

338

blind love

The greatest gift of love is to turn a blind eye. The most essential glue of any relationship is the ability of at least one of you to say, "I understand. It's okay. Let's just get on with things."

After all, that is what we continuously say to our own selves out of our self-love. And it is what we would like the One Above to say to us.

339

love pulleys

What is the way to bring a person closer to Torah—
whether it be your friend, your spouse, your child, or a
complete stranger?

It is not with rebuke, not with arguments, not with
intellectual games—but by pulling hard with thick cords
of love, by showing your faith in who he or she is, and
with real deeds to prove it.

340

man & woman

Look deeply and you will see that the Torah does not know of man and woman as separate beings. Each act is performed once through a single body—a body that in our world may appear as two, but which the Torah sees as one.

On the contrary, for both to do the same mitzvah would be redundant, for why should one half of the body do what the other has already done?

They are a single whole, whether they know of one another or not.

341

two minds

The mind of a woman and the mind of a man are two distinct minds at their very core. And only with both can there be a world.

It began when G-d decided to create a world. In doing so, He took two perspectives. He saw the world from beyond, as its Creator. And He saw the world from within, as the energy of life.

From that first perspective originates the mind of man; from the second, the mind of woman.

That is why the man has the power to conquer and subdue, but he does not have the woman's sense of the other.

That is why the woman feels the other. She does not conquer, she nurtures. But her light is tightly constrained.

As they bond together, the man unleashes the woman's light, and the woman teaches the man to feel the other. In that union shines the very essence of all that is holy and divine.

342

transfusion

A king without a queen, the *Zohar* says, is neither great nor a king. For it is the woman who empowers the man to conquer.

And it is the man who empowers the woman to nurture.

And then the man will learn from this woman that he, too, can reach within others and provide nurture.

And the woman will learn that through nurture, she can conquer.

343

she made him good

Before Woman was created, G-d said, "It is not good that Man is alone" (Genesis 2:18).

Once He made Woman, everything He made was very good.
—Midrash Tehillim 59:2

If so, how is it possible that a man could despise the woman who took him from not good to very good?

344

ignoring faults

Until after the final redeemer arrives, there is no person on earth without some fault. Where one person fails on one count, another fails elsewhere.

We don't appreciate someone else prying into our faults and underlining each one with a red pencil. So we know it is not right to do the same with another.

This is the way all people must relate to one another. This is especially so when it comes to your spouse and the parent of your children.

re-uniting

When man and woman were first formed, they were a single being.

Then G-d divided them apart, so that they could achieve a higher union.

Why is it higher?

Because now it is through their own effort.

That is true oneness: When two choose to be one.

346

getting personal

When does the depth of a relationship become realized? Once it has broken down.

As long as each fulfills the other's expectations, we see only a contract and its transactions. Once trust is breached, a new depth must appear: The depth of the human being.

If there is truly a relationship—if it is the person inside that matters— then there is a search for forgiveness, for return, and for healing.

So it was that within forty days of entering into a contract with the One Above, the Children of Israel broke the deal. And the soul below and the One Above discovered they could not part from one another.

347

forgiveness by the book

When his people broke the deal and incurred divine wrath, Moses told G-d, "Forgive them. And if you do not, erase me from Your book that You have written."

Meaning: "I know You want to forgive them. You love them no matter what. You loved them before, when they had all but abandoned You in Egypt, and You love them now as well. It's only this book that stands in the way. And if so, I want no part of such a book."

It was then that G-d wrote forgiveness into His book.

And so must we.

348

a different peace

True peace is not a forced truce, not a
homogenization of differences, not a common
ground that abandons our home territories.

True peace is the oneness that sprouts from
diversity, the beauty that emerges from a panorama
of colors, strokes, and textures, from the harmony
of many instruments each playing a unique part,
not one overlapping the other's domain by even the
breadth of a hair.

Those who attempt to blur those borders, whatever
be their motives, are unwittingly destroying the
world.

Beginning with the crucial border between man and
woman. For this is the beginning of all diversity, the
place where G-d's oneness shines most intensely
from within His precious world.

349

constant bonding

Matter and energy are two opposites. Energizing a piece of matter requires a constant flow.

Existence and nothingness are two opposites. Keeping the world in existence demands a constant renewal.

Heaven and earth are two opposites. Infusing the earthly with spirituality requires a constant effort.

Woman and man are two opposites. Therefore, courtship never ends.

350

reality in untidy boxes

Tell me you found G-d in a tidy package—I will tell you that it is not G-d, it is a product of a clever mind.

Tell me you found G-d in the limitless beyond—beyond space, beyond time. That too is not G-d. That is just a greater mind.

Where the boundless dwells within a bounded space, where darkness shines, silence sings, bitterness is sweet, and a moment lives forever, where a man and a woman live in harmony, an adult learns from a child, a warrior spreads kindness, and enmity subsides to make room for friendship and love,
where the body embraces the soul
and the soul the body,
in the union of all opposites—

there is G-d; there is the essence of all that is real.

351

fluid movement

We are all connected, like a single, fluid mass, and this is why we are able to help each other change. When one of us begins moving forward, everyone else is pulled along.

But if you yourself are standing still, how can you expect to push someone else ahead?

If you need to help someone else overcome his fault, first find that flaw within you. Move forward in that area, and then you can pull along the other guy.

352

dissatisfied on purpose

So you are not happy with the way things are in your world, your community, your house, your own self.

Who says things were designed to make you happy? G-d Himself is dissatisfied with all of it. He made such a world and put you here within it to do your part in fixing it.

Be strong and take on a load, and rejoice that soon will be a world that you had a hand in building.

353

friction

Our souls are the finishing tools for His handiwork.

They are the plows He applies to the harsh earth so it will absorb the rains from heaven, the sandpaper to grind away the coarse surfaces of life, the polishing-cloth so that it will glimmer in the light from above.

That friction that wears us down, those sparks that fly—it is the resistance to this refining process.

And if you should ask, how could it be that G-d's own creation should present resistance to His infinitely powerful breath?

In truth, it cannot. But He condenses that breath into a soul, He tightly focuses her power, until the harshness of this world can seem real to her, and then she will struggle, and in that struggle she will make the world shine.

354

healthy space

So obsessed with his own self and his own space, he fits each person into a rigid box to suit his egocentric world. Those who fit are friends. Those who don't are called all sorts of names.

Healthy human space flows and mixes. It has room for a thousand others.

355

the path of the humble

If we were truly humble, we would not be forever searching in higher paths on the mountaintops. We would look in the simple places, for the practical things that need to be done.

True, where do these simple, practical things reside? In a transient world, a world of falsehood, a world where people believe they have needs that are not real needs, where they suffer more pain than life truly creates.

In a world where your motives are always in question, where the difference you make is always in doubt. Because it is a world where you cannot give without gaining more than you have given, you cannot love without being loved, you cannot honor without being honored.

Nevertheless, the soul who knows her place knows that this is where the great and lofty G-d can most be found—in a simple act of lending a hand or a whispering a comforting word in a world of falsehood and delusions.

356

imaginary kindness

Most of the favors we do for others are things they do not need, things they only imagine they need, because they live in a world propelled by fantasies.

And most of the kindness we do is saturated with ulterior motives. We do kindness for those we love, those close to us, or those who make us feel good when they receive.

But this does not matter. They are acts of kindness, nonetheless, and G-d desires to be found in acts of kindness. And where can kindness be performed? In a world of delusions, where people imagine all sorts of needs, and each of us is dependent on the other.

The highest, indeed, is found in the lowest, the deepest truths are submerged in the muddiest pits of confusion.

357

community

This is a community: What one is lacking, the other fills in, so that together we make a perfect whole.

And this is what is needed to make a healthy community: That each of us recognize that we are lacking, and that we need the other to make us whole.

358

together

Even if all the Jewish people worshipped idols, but lived together in peace, the Sages taught, G-d could not punish them.

All the more so when they are united in a good cause— that oneness is a receptacle wide enough for open miracles.

359

we can heal the world

How can we heal the world? By being one.

What does it mean to be one?

If, wherever you go, you carry there every other Jew in your heart, then all of us are one.

And when we are one, all the peoples of the world can live in harmony as one.

And then the world is healed. For we are the heart of the world.

360

jewish unity

The first thing needed to fix the world is that Jews should love each other and be united. And this can begin even without a planning committee and without funding. It can begin with you.

out in the world

Who is going to fix up this mess of a world? The politicians? The social workers? The philosophers? The think tanks and analysts?

Perhaps some great minds can shed some light so we can find the door. Perhaps some sensible bureaucrat may even leave the door unlocked.

But don't wait for real change to enter through that door. Don't wait for the academics and authorities in their ivory and steel towers to plan or enforce it. Don't wait for those taking notes on the other side of a one-way glass to fix the world.

Real change is an inside job. It is made by those who have an investment in the real world. By people who are charging for their services, buying and selling, inventing and manufacturing, trading and transporting. Those building the world have the power to fix it.

◆

Money and *tikun* have much to do with one another. Both are about putting things together. Or people together. Or people and things together.

Somehow, just with those connections, you've created more value in the world. Since you created it, you get a major chunk of that value, often in the form of money.

It turns out that making money is magical—something out of nothing.

How does the magic work? Where does that value come from?

Go back to the idea of *tikun*. Everything began as a single thought. When we make connections, we are reassembling that thought. As the connections assemble, more and more meaning appears.

We see that meaning as value. Sometimes we can even represent that value as money. And with that money, we can make yet more connections.

It turns out that commerce, as well as art, music, literature, the sciences—basically all activities that are particular to the human race—can be a form of *tikun*. They all provide opportunities to connect the shattered fragments of our world to create value.

Now look at our world today. A global communications network in the hands of almost everyone has increased abundance many times over, spreading it to the extreme frontiers of human settlement.

For thousands of years, only a select few—around 5%—were literate. Today 80% of adults around the globe can read and write. Poverty and hunger have diminished worldwide more rapidly than anyone predicted—by more than 50% in twenty years. Despite the common perception, we enjoy the most peaceful era of history—because we've discovered it's better to make commerce than war.

A villager in Botswana may not have electricity, running water, or even a bicycle to ride, but he has a mobile phone, and with that, access to all human knowledge and a means to contribute yet more information and experience. Nothing could more powerfully transform a person's understanding of himself and his relationship to the world.

Connections are being made. Connections that create value.

The problem is that there are other kinds of connections. Connections, paradoxically, that tear us apart.

Tikun is what occurs when people do the things that people do—and do them right. It happens when we connect from the inside-out. When we deal with other people as fellow human beings. When we appreciate the value of the resources we work with. When we take pride in our services. Even more so when we see our work as a divine mission—which it truly is.

When business is not about value, but about money; not about the fruit, but about the shell; not about the people, but about what you can get out of them—then it's a dark and nasty force of chaos, dehumanization, and destruction.

Instead of harmonizing society, so that each makes his or her unique contribution, it renders a granulated, homogenized pseudo-culture—a world where all the traditional bonds of family, community, tribe, and culture are ripped away, to be replaced with isolation, abuse, and emptiness. We are left as chaff in the wind, to be swept in aimless, lonely circles. Nothing sticks, there is no center, there is no value.

So it is that history travels in two opposing trajectories at once, both driven by the same human drive to dominate our world—for better, but too often, for worse.

Who chooses which trajectory will dominate? Not the legislators. Not the academics. Not the preachers. Not the enlightened souls who sit and ponder.

It is the salesperson who sells his customers what he knows to be best for them. The school teacher who treats each child as a person, an entire world. The business executive who is concerned for the welfare of the company's employees both at the office back home and in the factory across the sea—and in the villages in which those workers live. The manufacturer whose every worker feels a sense of mission and meaning in their work.

Where the real world happens, from there is its *tikun*.

There will come a time, writes Maimonides, when "the occupation of the entire world will be only to know G-d." Meaning, we will have occupations. We will be builders. Importers. Exporters. Manufacturers. Professionals. And why will we occupy ourselves with these things? Because these are the ways to know the One who spoke and brought all things into being.

And so they are, as well, today.

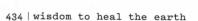

361

world

There are only three things on which your
mind must focus:

The One Above,
you below,
and the interface between the two of you—
the world and all it contains.

Invest yourself within the reality of your
world, and from there you will redeem
G-d's presence.

362

business transformation

There is a beast inside. It awaits you for its *tikun*.

How do you fix up the human beast? First with prayer, then with food, but ultimately by doing business.

You need to start with meditation and prayer, because that beast inside needs to experience not only wonder, but even love for G-d. The problem is, in prayer and meditation, you have not yet met that beast on its own ground.

Next, eat your breakfast like a human being is meant to eat—a step higher than the food you consume, raising it up rather than letting it pull you down. Then, yes, you have met your human beast on its own ground. But not on its own terms. You are still fighting with it—against its desire to be pulled down into the food.

So then go out into the world and provide goods and services of value, and do that with integrity.

No longer are you fighting against the human beast. You are working with it and from within it, with all the talents and skills you have. Because otherwise, you are not providing the value for which others are paying, and that is not integrity.

Now you can understand why the very first question asked of the soul when she returns from her mission in this world is not "How did you pray?" or "How did you eat" but "Did you do business with integrity?" For that is when you truly fixed up this world.

joseph

*And there came a day, and Joseph went to do his
work...* —*Genesis 39:11*

Joseph went to review his accounting books.
—*Targum Onkelos*

*Joseph, the tzaddik, went to review his accounting
books?!* —*Torat Chaim, Vayeishev*

Joseph was a soul from the World of Atzilut—a divine world
of pure light entirely beyond any physical or spiritual reality.
A world one with its Emanator.

For Joseph, even as he lived within a body within this world,
there was no world, because the light of his soul shone so
brightly, nothing of this world could exist.

And yet, here Joseph is going to do his work, to review his
accounting books!

It is one thing to be beyond the world, but to be so far beyond
and yet occupied with it, both at once—that is something
absolutely wondrous.

364

working lessons

If all the world is a classroom and all of life is
a lesson, then certainly your profession and
workplace are included.

After all, He has unlimited ways to provide your
livelihood—why did He direct you to this way of life?

What sparks of the divine await you here?

365

financial planning

Here is how to make an honest living, with confidence and minimal worry:

Determine how much you need to provide for your family needs.

Next, get into a business that can make that sum of money.

Now, put your best foot forward to do whatever needs to be done.

But no more than that. More will get you less.

Then pray for compassion, and trust in the One who provides all life to provide your livelihood as well.

You've put out just the right size bucket in the rain. Now trust that heaven will fill it to the brim.

366

worldly occupation

Why must we have jobs? Why can't our bread fall from heaven?

It does. Our bread is manna from heaven. But it bursts forth from Above like a solar flare—a light far too intense for any world to contain.

So, in each world in the chain of spiritual worlds that extend from above to below until our earthly realm, the beings of that world must labor to absorb that light. Only then can the light descend to the world that follows theirs in the chain—and there yet another form of labor is required, according to the limitations of that world.

Until the light arrives at our world. And here we must do the work that our world requires so that it, too, may absorb the light.

And that is why we each have our worldly occupations.

367

free buckets

Sometimes, not only the rain, but your buckets as well, are handed
to you from above.

Sometimes it's taken out of your hands to determine where
you should go, what you should do, and how it should be done.
Sometimes you are Joseph, captured and tied to a destiny too
great for you to fathom.

Sometimes you need to be quiet and just do what needs to be done.
Do the best with whatever you're given—honestly and earnestly.
And put your confidence in your real Employer.

368

misappropriation of funds

Each of us is allocated from above just the amount of time we need to get our mission done. Some of that time will be for learning, teaching and helping others. Some of that time will be needed for making a living—also a divine task with purpose and meaning.

But none of us can justify our obsession with making a living by claiming that it leaves no time to learn or to teach.

This is nothing less than misappropriation of funds— spending all the allotted time on one task at the expense of your principal purpose in this world. Each of us is foremost a student and a teacher.

369

reliance

Every step along the way, keep one thing in mind: The same G-d who runs the big, wide world is without a doubt the same G-d who runs the little world of each one of us.

Just as He knows what is going on in the macrocosmos, so He is well aware of what is happening in your microcosmos. And you can rely on Him to direct it for the good.

It is up to you not to mess things up. And how can a person mess up G-d's plans? By stubbornly grasping the wheel, as though you alone are the captain of the ship.

370

synergy

Not only is there is no conflict between your work and your time for study, meditation, and prayer—on the contrary, they complement one another:

When you start your day connecting it to Torah, it shines and all its parts hum in synchronicity.

And when you work honestly, because you carry the morning's inspiration in your heart, your work itself reveals to you divine providence before your open eyes.

371

sharing the workload

In every venture, divide the workload between yourself and your Partner Above.

Where is the dividing line? That depends on the sort of venture.

When it comes to anything to do with money, health, or anything material, the dividing line is that point at which you become emotionally obsessed. Up until there, do your job as best you know how. Anything necessary past that line is best left in His trust.

In spiritual matters, take whatever He gives you and fire it up with all you've got.

friends in time of need

G-d is with me among my helpers.

—Psalms 118:7

Your best friends are those who are at your side in times of distress.

And why are they there? Because you are at their side at the time of their distress.

Sometimes your charitable donations are seriously threatened. You might be short on funds, or the market might be unstable. Yet, nevertheless, you still provide with a full and generous hand.

You have stood by a good friend at an hour of distress. A friend called charity.

Sometimes, your fixed time for Torah study is under existential threat. You might be running off to business, chasing another client—and instead you stick it out to the end.

You have stood by a good friend at a threatening hour. A friend called Torah.

Without a doubt, such dear friends will not leave your dedication unrequited. When you will need them, they will come running.

373

simple advice

Ask advice from those with experience.

They will provide you freely that which they acquired at great expense.

374

two paths, two miracles

Two miracles, as related in the Talmud (*Taanit* 21a) and elaborated upon many times by the Rebbe:

On his travels, Rabbi Akiva took a donkey to free him from carrying his load, a rooster to wake him up early, and a lamp to study by night. (The Rebbe would comment at this point that this is in contradistinction to the general custom today to take a credit card and a toothbrush.)

Rabbi Akiva was a great sage who taught, among other things, that everything the All-Merciful does is for the good.

Once the All-Merciful arranged for Rabbi Akiva to arrive at a town where no one would provide lodging. He told himself it is all for the good and slept in the woods outside.

That night was full of disaster. When Rabbi Akiva sat down to study by the light of his lamp, a gust of wind blew it out. "Nu," he said, "everything the All-Merciful does is for the good"—and he lay down to sleep. After all, his rooster would wake him at the first hint of dawn.

But then, a fox attacked his rooster and ran off with it between his jaws. "Everything," Rabbi Akiva said, "is for the good." And he fell asleep.

It was the middle of the night when the donkey ended up prey to a lion. Rabbi Akiva mourned for the donkey, but he rejoiced at the great good that—somehow, in some way—was being done for him. And he fell back into a deep sleep.

In the morning he woke to find that an army had attacked the town and taken all its inhabitants captive.

"See," he said, "everything was for the good. Had I slept in the town, had my lamp burned, my rooster crowed or my donkey brayed, I would have been a target for the same pillagers who attacked that town!"

Rabbi Akiva saw it was for the good—but he did not see the good within the events themselves. He only saw that through these unfortunate events he was saved from a yet more unfortunate one...

One of Rabbi Akiva's teachers was a man named Nachum of Gamzu. "Gam zu" was a place, but it also means "even this." Nachum always would repeat the words, "Even this is for the good."

One time, the Jews found it necessary to send a chest of precious stones to the caesar. They chose to send Nachum, since all recognized that he lived a life filled with miracles. All the way to Rome, Nachum guarded the chest with his life. But on the last leg of the journey, an innkeeper surreptitiously exchanged the precious stones for sand. By the time Nachum discovered the ploy, it was too late to turn back. So he happily exclaimed, "This is fantastic! I shall do my job as emissary of the Jewish People, and G-d will fill in the rest!"—and he continued his way to the caesar.

"Your majesty," he proclaimed before the royal throne, "The Jews send you a gift!" And he opened the chest of sand. Nobody was very impressed. When the caesar announced that he would put him to death for his "mockery," Nachum joyously repeated his saying, "Even this is for the good!"

374 cont'd

That's when the miracle occurred: One of the caesar's advisors (actually Elijah the Prophet in disguise) suggested that this sand may have magical powers. "After all," he explained, "Abraham, the forefather of the Jews, vanquished four kings and their armies using magical sand that turned into arrows when thrown."

The caesar agreed to test it—and the Romans had no lack of wars to experiment with. The sand was issued to the Roman legions, and before long, news of a great, miraculous victory was reported. Nachum was released and abundantly rewarded. He was delighted—but not the least bit surprised.

(By the way, the innkeeper got his own in the end. You see, when he got wind of the story, the poor fool also came to Rome, pulling a wagon load of his plain, ordinary sand for the Roman legions....)

Unlike Rabbi Akiva, for Nachum of Gamzu all these events were not just for the good, they were good. They seemed disastrous, but that was just an artifact of a limited perspective. Nachum, however, had a higher perspective.

Today, we see suffering and pain—and we must do whatever we can to fix that. But we are on the verge of a whole new world. Such a new world, of such a higher perspective, that we will look back and see all that occurred in an entirely new light. Not only was it all worthwhile, it was truly good, all good.

375

miraculous obstacles

The paradigm of all obstacles is the Sea of Reeds. Only six days earlier, the Children of Israel had fled their slavery, but now an impasse stood before them, with Pharaoh and his army charging from behind.

But the greatest of barriers turned into the greatest of miracles. Not only did the sea become an ambush for the enemy, it also became a path that led the Children of Israel to their ultimate freedom.

So it is with every obstacle. When you're out to do the right thing, the entire world is there to assist you—including the most formidable threats and the most impossible challenges. The bigger they are, the more impossible to traverse, the greater the miracle they will provide.

That is the true reality of everything in this world: to serve you on your mission. What is your mission? To make this world miraculous.

And obstacles are miracles waiting to happen.

376

wall street idol

The ancients looked up at the heavens and gazed at the stars in their constellations. They honored them as stewards of divine energy and life, as the embodiment of all forces of nature and the origin of human passions.

They were wise, but they were fools—they abandoned the Master for the servant. For in truth there is only One and all else is but a tool in His hand.

Modern man looks up to the headlines of the finance page and sees there all the forces that will make or break his career, his retirement plans, his success as a human being.

He, too, is a fool, for in truth there is only One and all else is but a tool in His hand.

377

spirituality in time and space

Spiritual people tend to disdain all interaction with this world and strive to minimize it at all costs.

Torah enables a spiritual person to engage the world in real-time and real-space, and find there all for which his soul thirsts.

378

our land

The nations cannot understand why the Jewish people should have a land.

"If it is G-d and scriptures and religion that you are all about," they claim, "then why do you want a piece of earth? Will you find G-d in settling land? In governing a country? In defending territory? Is G-d in a certain place and not in another? Make up your mind! Is it heaven you want, or a plot of earth?"

Those words, perhaps, are never said. They are tacit words, engraved within the human psyche. And they are the bias behind all their contentions with us: We don't belong here, on earth, where they belong, playing by their rules. Because G-d is in the heavens, and the earth belongs to humankind.

But this is the mission of the Jewish people: for all to see that the same G-d in heaven is here within the earth, within all the endeavors of humankind, within all of human history. For there is nothing else but Him.

Beginning with that specific, well-defined, very special piece of earth to which our destiny is tied.

379

exchange of matter

Separating between your physical needs and your spiritual needs is both counter-productive and futile. The spiritual breathes life into the physical, and the physical rises to become spiritual in a perpetual chemistry of exchange.

Heal the soul and the body is renewed. Heal the body and the soul is empowered.

380

community and the individual

A community that builds itself by quashing the individual is not a community.

True unity and harmony is only achieved when each individual plays his or her unique part, meshing and interlocking together as a single, organic whole.

381

worldly blessings

G-d promises the Jewish nation that if they will all be keeping His *mitzvot* and toiling in its study, the trees will bear their fruits in their seasons, and the earth will yield its bounty.

But is this the reward for keeping *mitzvot*? Is this the reward of those who toil to understand it?

Rather, He is telling us, "See how essential is my Torah to the very fabric of existence. It is not just wisdom—it is the essence of all things. You sit and toil to bring its light into your world, and as that light enters, the trees bear their fruits in their season, and the earth yields its bounty!"

382

wise contraptions

From everything, there is something to learn.

When the telephone was first introduced, a wise man was asked, "What can we learn from this contraption?"

He answered, "That which is spoken here is heard there."

So they asked, "And from the telegraph?"

He replied, "Every word costs."

"And from the train?"

"Hesitate for a moment, and you could lose the whole journey."

383

the experiment

Go...from your land, from your birthplace and from
your father's house, to the land that I will show you.
—Genesis 12:1

Life is an experiment. You are the subject.

We begin with a hypothesis. Then we devise a test. But one test is
not sufficient. We have to test our hypothesis under multiple and
diverse conditions. If in each situation the same result occurs, only
then can we say we have discovered a truth.

So, too, with the truth within you. Staying in one safe and
comfortable situation throughout your life and remaining a good
boy or girl is no big deal.

But when the earth keeps shifting beneath your feet, the seasons
carry you from one extreme to the other, and every day demands
a mode of life distinct from the day before, only then can you
discover the truth you hold.

384

the source

People imagine we believe that Abraham and Moses gave the world the ideas of morality and value of life.

It is not true. These ideas were known to Adam and to Noah. It is just that, with time, humankind had mostly forgotten them.

What these giants brought to the world was a greater idea: That the values essential to humanity's survival can only endure when they have a larger context; when we understand ourselves as created beings engaged by the Master of this Universe to take care of His world.

385

getting real

To know that this world is not some wild jungle where whoever is stronger or richer or smarter can abuse and destroy without regard for those beneath them—this is not a matter of religion or faith, particular to one people or group of believers. This is the underlying reality—that this world has a Master, and that Master is not any of us.

A peaceful society can only endure when it is built upon that which is real and true.

epilogue

By the seventh generation of Chabad, the walls separating the Jew from the rest of the world had all come tumbling down. It was 1951, and the Rebbe, Rabbi Menachem M. Schneerson, accepted the leadership with these words: "We are the generation to complete the work of all the generations before us, to finally bring heaven down to earth."

Until this point, Chabad had been about the soul, the mind and the heart. That was the material world that needed to be fixed.

For the Rebbe, fixing up the material world meant the entire big world out there, every last country, every last culture, every last individual. You could almost say that everything up to this point had been only a rehearsal—battle practice for the final victory. And now, the paratroopers were landing on foreign soil. Everywhere.

It meant sending young couples and their children out to every place a Jew may roam—whether that be Tunisia or Thailand,

Kathmandu or Kentucky. What Rabbi Schneur Zalman of Liadi, the Baal Shem Tov, and the Ari had spoken in the esoteric language of the soul and the heavens suddenly meant here, now, down on this earth. *Tikun* had hit the hard, concrete pavement.

It wasn't just those Chasidic families. The Rebbe asked this of every Jew and every human being with whom he came in contact. The message, always: You have a job to do. The circumstances in which you find yourself, the community in which you live, your place of work and the skills and talents G-d has given you—they are all screaming out to you to do your job. And what is that job? To turn this world on its head.

Neither was the Rebbe satisfied with his impact on the Jewish world alone. He urged Jews to speak with their non-Jewish neighbors and acquaintances, to tell them, "You are created in the divine image. You have a divine mission to accomplish. We all have to increase our acts of goodness and kindness. That is all that's needed to bring the redemption of the entire world."

The transformation left many older Chasidim gasping in the dust. For over a century and a half, Chabad had been about theological contemplation and "labor of the heart." Now, the Rebbe introduced something the likes of which had never been seen before: A worldwide organization dedicated to reaching out to every Jew and pulling them back in.

Not that any of that contemplative, inner labor was ever left behind. It remains the curriculum of every Chabad student. It was simply extended outward, downward, and into the world.

An outside observer would explain simply: These were urgent times. Six million had been lost—even more in Russia—the rate of assimilation in the West was accelerating, and if something drastic wasn't done fast to save world Jewry, there wouldn't be any Jews left to save.

But if you stood at the Rebbe's *farbrengens*—the gatherings at 770 Eastern Parkway, where students and Chasidim would sit or stand for hours and listen to his talks, sing Chasidic melodies, say l'chaim, and listen some more—there you would pick up an entirely different story. The inside story.

"We are the last generation of this exile, the generation to greet Moshiach," the Rebbe would say. "We are gathering the very last sparks, the most concealed and tightly held. We are making the final touches, polishing the buttons. These are the last preparations for a world as it was meant to be. And to do that, you cannot stay within the four walls of your yeshivah or your synagogue. To do that, you must go out into the world, with all your essence and being, and there be a beacon of light, a gatherer of sparks."

Chabad is not two worlds; it is all one, and the only way it can be understood is as a single whole—albeit, working in two opposite directions: from the top-down and from the ground-up. Chabad is about bringing the highest light of the divine to every corner of G-d's world, and it is about discovering and redeeming the divine spark hidden within all that exists.

At one time, that was achieved only in the world of the spirit. In our times, it has become as literal as imaginable.

It's strange—what I am about to say was never stated explicitly, yet all who have been steeped in the Rebbe's world have tacitly understood the same thing. It was implied, again and again, from so many different angles. At some point, it has to be stated loud and clear.

Certainly, every human being on this planet has his or her role to fulfill in its *tikun*. But the Maker of All Souls deemed that a Jewish soul was meant to heal the world with the light of Torah. And that raises a great question. Because, if that is so, why would G-d toss such a soul into a world where she would have no idea that there could be anything spiritual or meaningful to discover in the whole of Judaism?

It could only be that this is the exclusive means to recover those final, lost sparks.

Like a homing pigeon sent on a journey to return with precious jewels, so the souls of Israel are scattered among the nations of the world, among every sort of ideology and idealism, lifestyle and compulsion, ashram and cult, rat-race and escapism. So deep must they plunge that it takes the army of a *tzaddik*, a battalion fighting with all its might, to pull them out of there, so they can bring those jewels back home.

Some sparks can be returned home with a simple mitzvah. Some can only be extracted by cracking a hard nut and tossing out a pile of trash. And some—those "tied down," as Rabbi Schneur Zalman described them—only by exerting every ounce of your strength to pull yourself out of their sticky mud.

There is a teaching that says this—almost:

> *The only reason G-d spread the Jewish People among the nations was so that they could gain converts. As the verse says, "I have planted you among the nations." If a man plants seed, does he not expect to reap a hundred bushels of seed for every bushel planted? (Judges 5:11)*
> —*Talmud Pesachim 87b*

Rabbi Schneur Zalman of Liadi asked, "Can we take this literally? How many converts have there been in history? Could we possibly be in exile from our land for 1,800 years for this reason alone? If this were meant literally, the world should be filled with Jews by now!"

"Rather," he answered, "the converts to which the Talmud refers are none other than the lost sparks. By spreading us out among the nations, we wrestle out those sparks from their place, on their own territory, so that their redemption is a real and lasting one."

Rabbi Schneur Zalman may have seen it, but how many others could have understood how far this would go, to what places we would have to journey to rescue those sparks, how deep those souls would have to plunge to find them, and what extreme means would be needed to convince the homing pigeons to return home.

In 1967, the Rebbe spoke about how the souls had begun to return home. In the 1980s, he talked about the walls of the exile crumbling before us. In 1991, he insisted that enough sparks had been gathered, and it was incomprehensible that the final *geulah* had not yet come.

It was up to us, he said, to complete the job—we had to want it from the innermost of our hearts, and demand it with sincerity. And in order for that to happen, we had to learn what *geulah* is, understand it and come to feel it as though we were living it already. He continued speaking that way until the day of his stroke, in 1992.

In each of our private lives, much work remains to be done. But the world is ready. It is we who must awaken a longing to come home.

If we would recognize what this world really is and who we really are, how high we could be and what a world we could be living in, how we are but silkworms trapped in the darkness of our cocoons, miners trapped in a cave so long that we have forgotten the light of day, a bright, glorious day that awaits us—we would be pounding our fists on heaven's door, demanding to see the fruits of our labor, demanding it now and no later.

In the meantime, keep working. Work hard. For we are G-d's partners in the creation of heaven and earth.

About Sources

This list provides sources from the talks, letters and other writings of the Rebbe and his predecessors for further study. It covers most, but not all the contents of this book.

As I wrote in the introduction, while this book contains few direct quotations, its content is firmly grounded in this material. If you are familiar with additional sources that may be useful to other readers, please consider contributing them by email to editor@chabad.org.

Tikun

1. Leave Nothing Behind
Torat Menachem—Hitvaaduyot 5713, vol. 3, pp. 88-89, and countless other instances.

2. What Can I Fix?
Likkutei Sichot, vol. 3, p. 1005; vol. 32, p. 152, on Shabbat 33b.

3. The Taller They Are...
Likkutei Sichot, vol. 15, p. 288, note 65.

4. Inside Job
See Shaarei Teshuvah, 50c ff. Sefer Hamaamarim 5627, p. 273; 5629, p. 186; 5659, p. 108; 5704, p. 106; Likkutei Sichot, vol. 25, pp. 193-203.

5. A Sign From Below
Reshimot, Issue 51.

6. If It's Broken...
Avot 2:16. Reshimot, Issue 44.

7. Top Down, Ground Up
Sefer Hamaamarim 5722, p. 68 ff. (also 5659, p. 148 ff; 5704, p. 66 ff; 5712, p. 171 ff.); Sefer Hamaamarim 5714, p. 113 ff.

8. Dual Peace
Sefer Hamaamarim 5722, p. 68 ff.

9. Redeemed in Peace
Sefer Hamaamarim 5722, p. 68 ff.

10. Tied to the Source
Likkutei Sichot, vol. 10, p. 100 ff.

11. Where You Cannot Go
Torat Menachem—Hitvaaduyot 5714, vol. 2, pp. 187-191.

12. Nothing Higher
Torat Menachem—Sefer Hamaamarim Melukat, vol. 4, p. 48 ff.

13. Choose Your Strategy
See Hayom Yom, 28 Menachem Av.

Radical Reversal

31. The Goal
Likkutei Sichot, vol. 3, pp. 976-977, fn. 19; ibid., vol. 5, pp. 62-63; Torat Menachem—Sefer Hamaamarim Bati Legani, vol. 1, p. 25 ff.

32. The Drama

33. The Game
Tanya, chs. 36-37. See also Torat Menachem—Hitvaaduyot 5714, vol. 1, p. 228 ff.

34. Cutting Off the Supply
Tanya, ch. 37.

35. Completion
Tanya, ch. 37.

36. Finally Winning
Sefer Hamaamarim 5710, pp. 131-132; Talk of Shabbat Beshalach 5741, sec. 37; Talk of Shabbat Ki Tavo 5741, sec. 58; Torat Menachem—Hitvaaduyot 5746, vol. 1, p. 87.

37. Longing For Spring
Torat Menachem—Hitvaaduyot 5746, vol. 1, pp. 536-537 ff.

38. Technology
Likkutei Sichot, vol. 15, pp. 42-48.

39. Treasure Island
Likkutei Sichot, vol. 15, p. 438; ibid. vol. 5, pp. 459-461.

40. Fearless
Likkutei Sichot, vol. 30, p. 234.

41. Redeeming Hope
Likkutei Sichot, vol. 30, pp. 182-183.

42. Pity on the Cosmos
Talk of 15 Shevat 5741, sec. 5.

43. Cosmic Marriage
Torat Menachem—Hitvaaduyot 5712, vol. 2, p. 151 ff.

44. The Ultimate Delight
Sefer Hamaamarim Bati Legani, vol. 1, pp. 28-29.

45. Earned Living

46. Hiding Destiny
Torat Menachem—Sefer Hamaamarim Melukat, vol. 1, p. 45.

47. Open Your Eyes
Sefer Hasichot, 5752, vol. 1, p. 152.

Darkness Speaks

Darkness speaks
Torat Menachem—Sefer Hamaamarim Melukat, vol. 3, p. 188 ff.; Likkutei Sichot, vol. 17, p. 92 ff.; Torat Menachem—Sefer Hamaamarim Bati Legani, vol. 1, p. 20 ff.

48. Freedom Out of Darkness
Torat Menachem—Sefer Hamaamarim Bati Legani, vol. 1, p. 20 ff.

49. The Choice
Torat Menachem—Sefer Hamaamarim Bati Legani, vol. 2, pp. 623-624 ff.; Torat Menachem—Sefer Hamaamarim Bati Legani, vol. 1, pp. 25-29; Torat Menachem—Sefer Hamaamarim Melukat, vol. 2, p. 115 ff.; ibid., p. 131 ff.

50. Faith in the Dark
Sefer Hamaamarim 5710, pp. 153-154; Torat Menachem—Sefer Hamaamarim Bati Legani, vol. 2, p. 594 ff.; ibid., p. 622 ff.

51. Light Meets Dark
Torat Menachem—Sefer Hamaamarim Melukat, vol. 4, p. 111 ff.

52. Balaam
Talk of 12 Tammuz, 5730, sec. 9; Talk of Shabbat Balak, 5730, sec. 4.

53. Trickle of Delight
Avot 4:17. Vekachah 5637, ch. 17.

54. Squeezed By the Barriers
Torat Menachem—Sefer Hamaamarim Melukat, vol. 4, p. 48 ff.

55. Melting Evil
Tanya, ch. 30; Likkutei Torah, Teitzei 35b-d ff.; Sefer Hamaamarim 5745, p. 273 ff.; Torat Menachem—Hitvaaduyot 5751, vol. 4, pp. 213, 227.

56. Internal Terrorism
Tanya, chs. 28, 30.

57. Conquest

58. Mixtures
From a letter.

59. Help From the Past
Torat Menachem—Sefer Hamaamarim Melukat, vol. 4, p. 121 ff.

60. Stop Groping

61. Rock Bottom
Torat Menachem—Sefer Hamaamarim Melukat, vol. 3, p. 44 ff.

62. Still Rock Bottom
Torat Menachem—Sefer Hamaamarim Melukat, vol. 3, p. 44 ff.

63. The Captive
Torat Menachem—Sefer Hamaamarim Melukat, vol. 4, p. 216 ff.

64. G-d Raw
Torat Menachem—Sefer Hamaamarim Melukat, vol. 4, p. 216 ff.

65. A Duel of Beasts
Torat Menachem—Sefer Hamaamarim Melukat, vol. 4, p. 216 ff., from Torat Chaim, Toldot 2c-d.

66. Duets
Shaarei Orah 25b; Shaarei Teshuvah 35b.

67. Lifted By the Past
Likkutei Sichot, vol. 17, p. 187.

68. Return With Love
Likkutei Sichot, vol. 17, p. 190.

69. Life Lives On
Torat Menachem—Sefer Hamaamarim Melukat, vol. 4, p. 138 ff.

70. Preconception
Likkutei Sichot, vol. 10, pp. 7-12.

71. The Bottomless Pit
Torat Menachem—Sefer Hamaamarim Melukat, vol. 2, p. 1 ff.

72. Light's Advantage
Torat Menachem—Sefer Hamaamarim Bati Legani, vol. 1, p. 20 ff.

73. Song and Silence

74. Poor reception
Iggeret Hakodesh, 11.

75. Deep Roots
Torat Menachem—Sefer Hamaamarim Melukat, vol. 3, p. 188 ff.

76. The Lost Ark
Likkutei Sichot, vol. 26, p. 156 ff.

77. Close & Dark
Sefer Hasichot 5752, vol. 1, pp. 157-158.

78. Demand Your Rights
Likkutei Sichot, vol. 30, pp. 182-183.

Meaning

Meaning
Sefer Hamaamarim 5710, pp. 111-112; Tanya, ch. 36; Yom Tov Shel Rosh Hashanah 5666, p. 1 ff.

79. G-d in Action
Torat Menachem—Sefer Hamaamarim Melukat, vol. 2, p. 86 ff.

80. Inside Workers
From a letter.

81. Beyond Sincerity
Tanya, ch. 38; Likkutei Sichot, vol. 15, p. 247; Torat Menachem—Sefer Hamaamarim Melukat, vol. 2, p. 17 ff.

The Now

Laughter, Bliss, Inner Joy

136. Reason to Celebrate

137. Stories of Life
Likkutei Sichot, vol. 14, p. 162; Sefer Hamaamarim 5716, p. 114 ff.

138. Explosive Joy
Maimonides, Hilchot Lulav 8:12; Likkutei Sichot, vol. 17, p. 275; Torat Menachem—Hitvaaduyot 5745, vol. 4, p. 2237.

139. Humble & Happy
Sefer Hamaamarim 5679, p. 91, cited and elucidated in Torat Menachem—Sefer Hamaamarim Melukat, vol. 1, p. 277 ff.

140. This Is Good
Likkutei Sichot, vol. 1, p. 284.

141. Not an Angel, Not a Beast
Tanya, ch. 27.

142. A Soft Stick
Hayom Yom, 28 Shevat; Torat Menachem—Hitvaaduyot 5716, vol. 3, p. 106 ff.; Igrot Kodesh, vol. 6, p. 157; ibid., vol. 10, p. 240.

143. Celebrating No Matter What

144. Joyful Emptiness
Sefer Hamaamarim 5718, p. 58; Torat Menachem—Hitvaaduyot 5723, vol. 2, p. 317 ff.

145. Dancing With Feet
Torat Menachem—Sefer Hamaamarim Melukat, vol. 1, p. 210 ff.; Likkutei Sichot, vol. 20, p. 267; ibid., p. 370.

146. Real Rich
Sefer Hamaamarim 5729, pp. 147 ff. and 267 ff.; Torat Menachem—Sefer Hamaamarim Melukat, vol. 4, p. 34 ff.

147. Unimaginable Journeys

148. The Echo Upstream
Hayom Yom, 13 Iyar; Likkutei Sichot, vol. 14, p. 403 (based on Zohar).

149. Infinite & Intimate
Torat Menachem—Sefer Hamaamarim Melukat, vol. 3, p. 315 ff.

150. Cursed and Blessed
Torat Menachem—Sefer Hamaamarim Melukat, vol. 3, p. 65 ff.

151. Realistic Optimism
Talk of 20 Cheshvan, 5741.

152. Take the High Road
Sefer Hamaamarim 5746, p. 64; Sefer Hasichot 5750, vol. 1, p. 27.

153. Confusing Body and Soul
Tanya, ch. 31.

154. The Highest Happiness
Likkutei Sichot, vol. 16, pp. 365-372.

Inner Wisdom

vol. 3, p. 113 ff.; Talk of the Night of
Simchat Torah 5736, secs. 5-7 and
countless other talks.

173. Diamonds and Emeralds
From a letter to Rabbi Jonathan Sacks
in his youth.

174. Illumination
Torat Menachem—Hitvaaduyot 5742,
vol. 3, p. 1626; ibid., 5748, vol. 4, p. 175.

175. Begin With Alef
Talk of the Night of Simchat Torah
5736, sec. 16.

176. What Is Alef?
Hayom Yom, 8 Adar I; Torat
Menachem—Hitvaaduyot 5716, vol. 2,
pp. 43-44.

177. Daily Refreshments
Torat Menachem—Sefer Hamaamarim
Melukat, vol. 4, p. 138 ff.

178. Torah and Us

179. Jewish Nucleus
From a letter.

180. Teaching Despite
Himself
Talk of 13 Tamuz 5736, sec. 4.

181. Holistic Study
From a letter.

182. Faithful Questions

183. Faithful Deeds

184. The Unlikely Pair
Torat Menachem—Hitvaaduyot 5721,
vol. 1, p. 309 ff.; Torat Menachem—Sefer
Hamaamarim Melukat, vol. 3, p. 127 ff.

185. Entering the Palace
Torat Menachem—Hitvaaduyot 5721,
vol. 1, p. 309 ff.; Torat Menachem—Sefer
Hamaamarim Melukat, vol. 3, p. 127 ff.

186. Creation, G-dliness,
G-d
Vekachah, ch. 78.

187. Paradise
Shmuot Vesippurim, vol. 3, p. 229. See
Kuntres Umaayan, Discourse 1, ch. 3.

188. Delight Unlocked
Sefer Hamaamarim 5696, pp. 8, 18, 21;
Likkutei Sichot, vol. 26, p. 207; Torat
Menachem—Hitvaaduyot 5745, vol. 4,
p. 2527.

189. Delight Condensed
Torat Menachem—Sefer Hamaamarim
Melukat, vol. 2, p. 411 ff.; Iggeret
Hakodesh, 29.

190. Traditions of the
Future
Likkutei Sichot, vol. 10, p. 162.

I & I

Help From Within

p. 1048 ff.; Torat Menachem—Sefer
Hamaamarim Melukat, vol. 4, p. 1 ff.

223. Spiritual Junkies and Hedonists
Torat Menachem—Hitvaaduyot 5722,
vol. 3, p. 90 ff.; Likkutei Sichot, vol. 4,
p. 1048 ff.; Torat Menachem—Sefer
Hamaamarim Melukat, vol. 4, p. 1 ff.

224. Even Higher
Igrot Kodesh vol. 7, p. 376; ibid., vol. 11
p. 421; Torat Menachem—Hitvaaduyot
5723, vol. 1, p. 124 ff.

225. Tuned In

226. Not With Toil

227. Slaying Monsters Together
Torat Menachem—Sefer Hamaamarim
Melukat, vol. 2, p. 73 ff.

228. Harsh or Kind
Sefer Hasichot 5751, vol. 1, p. 228,
citing Kedushat Levi.

229. Above as Below
Iggeret Hakodesh, 11. Likkutei Torah,
Chukat 62a.

230. The Ingenious Mudhole

231. Pull a Rope
Igrot Kodesh, vol. 6, p. 147.

232. Through a Darkened Lens
From a letter.

233. Traveling to Yourself
Torat Menachem—Sefer Hamaamarim
Melukat, vol. 1, p. 250 ff.

234. Not Listening

235. The Mentor

236. Finding an Angel
Torat Menachem—Hitvaaduyot 5747,
vol. 2, p. 632.

237. Personal Trainer
See Tanya, end of ch. 9; ibid., ch. 28.

238. No Bad Roads
Likkutei Sichot, vol. 5, pp. 66-67.

Fix the Beast

380 ff.; *Hayom Yom, 5 Sivan; Sefer Hamaamarim 5721, pp. 22-23.*

257. Fire From Heaven
Torat Menachem—Sefer Hamaamarim Melukat, vol. 3, p. 15 ff.

258. Truth For a Moment
Likkutei Sichot, vol. 17, p. 115; Torat Menachem—Hitvaaduyot 5728, vol. 1, p. 32 ff.; Torat Menachem—Sefer Hamaamarim Melukat, vol. 3, p. 217 ff.

259. Faith, Intellect & Wisdom
Tanya, ch. 35.

260. Intelligence, Liberated
Torat Menachem—Sefer Hamaamarim Melukat, vol. 3, p. 127 ff.

261. Grasping
Tanya, ch. 24.

262. Beyond Faith & Intellect
Torat Menachem—Hitvaaduyot 5721, vol. 1, p. 310 ff.; Torat Menachem—Hitvaaduyot 5751, vol. 2, p. 349;. Torat Menachem—Sefer Hamaamarim Melukat, vol. 3, p. 127 ff.

263. Faith and Reason
Likkutei Sichot, vol. 16, p. 245.

264. Head and Feet
Likkutei Sichot, vol. 15, p. 15.

265. Simple Thought
Hayom Yom, 19 Shevat.

266. Reciprocity
Torat Menachem—Sefer Hamaamarim 5720, pp. 111-112.

267. Half & Whole
Talk of Shabbat Pekudei 5741, secs. 61-62

268. Bad Packaging
Torat Menachem—Sefer Hamaamarim Melukat, vol. 2, p. 203 ff.; Kuntres Umaayan, Discourse 19, ch. 2.

269. Answers in Boxes
Torat Menachem—Sefer Hamaamarim Melukat, vol. 2, p. 203 ff.

270. Unwrapping
Torat Menachem—Sefer Hamaamarim Melukat, vol. 2, p. 203 ff.

271. The Paradox of Prayer

272. Let Him In

273. In His Presence
Torat Menachem—Sefer Hamaamarim Melukat, vol. 3, p. 127 ff.

274. Real Idols
Siddur Im Dach, Lulav.

275. True Lies
Likkutei Sichot, vol. 36, p. 196.

276. Does He Need Our Praises?
Torat Menachem—Sefer Hamaamarim Melukat, vol. 3, p. 276 ff.

Learn as a Child

Wonder

311. Sustained Wonder
Hayom Yom, 12 and 19 Cheshvan.

312. Splitting the Sea
Likkutei Sichot, vol. 3, p. 880.

313. Real Time
See Iggeret Hakodesh, 14. A theme in many of the Rebbe's farbrengens.

314. Walking Miracles
Torat Menachem—Hitvaaduyot 5745, vol. 2, p. 954; Rabbenu Bachya Ibn Paquda, Chovot Halevavot.

315. Being & Not Being

316. From Beyond, With Love
Torat Menachem—Sefer Hamaamarim Melukat, vol. 2, p. 99 ff. See also R. Yehuda Loew (Maharal), preface to Gevurot Hashem.

317. Change
Torat Menachem—Sefer Hamaamarim Melukat, vol. 4, p. 138 ff.

318. The Unnatural Nature of Things
Torat Menachem—Sefer Hamaamarim Melukat, vol. 2, p. 99 ff.; ibid., p. 107 ff.

319. Playing With Our Minds
Likkutei Sichot, vol. 6, p. 21, and sources cited in footnotes.

320. Delight and Quintessence
Likkutei Sichot, vol. 6, p. 22; Torat

Menachem—Sefer Hamaamarim Bati L'gani, vol. 1, pp. 135 ff. and 141 ff.

321. Engaged
Sefer Hamaamarim 5700, p. 5 ff.; Torat Menachem—Sefer Hamaamarim Melukat, vol. 3, p. 80 ff.

322. The Unknowable You
Torat Menachem—Sefer Hamaamarim Melukat, vol. 4, p. 103 ff.

323. Nature, Miracles & Beyond
Torat Menachem—Sefer Hamaamarim Melukat, vol. 2, p. 99 ff.

324. Mystery By Design
Torat Menachem—Sefer Hamaamarim Melukat, vol. 2, p. 99 ff.

325. Simple Purpose
Iggeret Hakodesh, 11.

Healing Begins At Home

Out in the World

*Menachem—Hitvaaduyot 5713, vol. 1,
p. 176.*

383. The Experiment
*Torat Menachem—Hitvaaduyot 5749,
vol. 1, p. 316.*

384. The Source

385. Getting Real
*Torat Menachem—Hitvaaduyot 5746,
vol. 1, p. 407 ff.*

about the Lubavitcher Rebbe

The Lubavitcher Rebbe, Rabbi Menachem M. Schneerson, was heir to a line of Chasidic Masters that began with the towering figure of the Baal Shem Tov and carried it into the modern day.

With the passing of his father-in-law, Rabbi Yosef Yitzchak Schneersohn, in 1950, after an entire year of petitions and pressure, he accepted the mantle of leadership of what remained of the Chabad-Lubavitch Chasidic sect—a small group of those who had survived the inferno of the Holocaust and the religious persecution of Soviet Russia. Immediately he began to send agents to assist Jewish communities worldwide. In the sixties, he saw in the prevailing spirit of non-conformity, a spiritual reawakening. Through his work, tens of thousands of Jews returned to their roots and their spiritual heritage, as thousands of institutions were established in every part of the globe.

People of all faiths and walks of life travelled from afar to seek his advice and hear his wisdom. Politicians, civil rights activists, writers, scientists, religious leaders, scholars, business people, and any person who sought wisdom and guidance, lined up at his door for many hours every week. Sacks of mail arrived daily with requests for guidance and blessings from every corner of the world.

His talks and letters covered a wide gamut of topics, from the most esoteric teachings of Kabbalah and the nuances of Talmudic debate to his concerns over public school education in America and the safety of those living in Israel. In his signature style, everything had to have a practical application.

In 1978, on his 76th birthday, Congress proclaimed Rabbi Schneerson's birthday as, "Education Day, USA," and subsquently awarded the Rebbe the National Scroll of Honor.

In 1995, the Rebbe was posthumously awarded the Congressional Gold Medal, an award granted to only 130 Americans since Thomas Jefferson, for "outstanding and lasting contributions."

This book offers every person an opportunity to connect with the Rebbe through his teachings, condensed from over 50 years of letters, public talks, private conversations, and written works, presented in an accessible format.

about the author

Rabbi Tzvi Freeman was born in Vancouver, Canada, where he became involved at an early age in Yoga, Tao, and radical politics. In 1975, he left a career as a classical guitarist and composer to study Talmud and Jewish mysticism for nine years.

He is a senior editor at Chabad.org, for which he writes the *Daily Dose of Wisdom*, from which the meditations of this volume were extracted. He also directs the Chabad.org *Ask-the-rabbi* team and produces *Kabbala Toons*, a series of short, animated videos starring Rabbi Infinity.

His other books include:
- Bringing Heaven Down To Earth, Book I
- Bringing Heaven Down To Earth, Book II
- Heaven Exposed
- Men, Women & Kabala
- Trembling With Joy

Dedicated in honor of
Yitzak Isaac ben Yenta Basha

Alexander, **Benjamin** and **Isaac**: Choose to live, learn and laugh, always. Health, happiness, purpose, love and spirit.

Love Mom and Dad—Genia and Stewart Taub

Dedicated in memory of my son whose Neshama was too large for his vessel and quickly fulfilled its purpose.
It was an honor and privilege to be Gregory (Mordechai) Singer's mother.

In Memory of Freddy Efraim Mashaal Ben Menashi & Simha
from his Wife Danielle and Gabriel & Menashi

For my brother: Alexander M. Sterling.

May your mouth's words and heart's meditation inspire the reader to do his part to repair the world and return to it the One you are channelling.

לז"נ אבותי משה אברהם בן אהרן ליב ולאה בת ליב

Lovingly dedicated to the memory of Mr. Lev Bashmachnikov

In honor of Lori Sandra Katz and David Jonathan Katz and family.
In gratititude for all their support. With a heart full of love, Mom.
In memory of my beloved parents, Dr. Haskell and Rosalie Sterling.

In loving memory of our beloved father and husband,
Stefan Simcha Bunem ben Avraham Z"L

Dedicated to the blessings of our children Daniel and Ji-Hae, Lesley and Eitan, Ted and Alisa and Kenny and our grandchildren Harvey, Lily, Marcus, Charlie, Lyla, and Livia.

Kol Hakavod Rabbi Freeman. With lovel, Arbess Family NYC.

Our beautiful Children, Ori, Leetal and Joshi that we love unconditionally and to eternity. May you all live your lives with Torah and Yiddishkeit with generation after generation! Love, Mom and Dad!

In memory of Sylvia & Sylvan Zemel

For the merit, blessings and success of Robert Isaac & Lizette Elias and Family

לע"נ ר' יהודא ליב בן הר' יצחק ע"ה — נפטר ח' תמוז ה'תשע"ז ת.נ.צ.ב.ה.

May Hashem grant us all peace, happiness, wealth and good health. The Talit family.

Dedicated by Pasquale D'Alesio

In loving memory of Joseph Omansky and Lou Omansky

In memory of Jose Alfredo Hernandez Lopez

In honor of my parents, Bernard and Marjorie Schneider. Love conquers all.

May the wisdom of Tikun Olam—to heal the earth—
spread widely with compassion to all living things.
"The earth and all that fills it, are G-d's."